Miss Ruby's
SOUTHERN CREOLE
& CAJUN CUISINE

With a Foreword by the
Honorable Lindy Boggs

by Miss Ruby Wilkenson

Peanut Butter Publishing
Seattle, Washington

Other than mutual admiration, there is no connection between Miss Ruby's Restaurant in New Orleans and Miss Ruby's Cafe at 135 Eighth Avenue in New York City. The latter is owned by Ruth Adams Bronz, author of *Miss Ruby's American Cooking,* published in 1989 by Harper & Row.

Cover Design: Graphiti Associates, Inc.
Illustrations: Richard Hunter
Photography: Poissenot Production
Typesetting: Grafisk Design

Copyright © 1990 by Ruby Wilkinson
All rights reserved. Printed in the United States of America
ISBN 0-89716-350-8

Published by Peanut Butter Publishing
200 Second Ave. W.
Seattle, WA 98119
(206) 281-5965

Distributed by:
Acropolis Books Ltd.
11741 Bowman Green Dr.
Reston, VA 22090

Warehouse and Customer Service:
Acropolis Books Ltd.
13950 Park Center Road
Herndon, VA 22071

❦ Contents

❦ Dedication

To my daughter Jean, for her support and diligent help for five years.
She was my manager, day-time chef and pastry chef.
All our famous and delicious desserts are her creations.
Without her, this recipe book would never have become a reality.

❦ Acknowledgements

The cover of this book was photographed in Miss Ruby's French Quarter garden.

All color photographs are by Loyd Poissenot of Poissenot Production, Dallas, Texas.

Food styling is by Wayne Miller, New Orleans, Louisiana.

Make-up and hair design by J. Burke Saucier of Albert Brown Salons.

Fashions by Roger Johns, Ltd. and Yvonne LeFleur of New Orleans.

Pen and ink illustrations by Richard Hunter of New Orleans.

My thanks to the following:

The Honorable Lindy Boggs, member of Congress, for writing the Foreword.

Leslie J. Rossouw, B.Sc., Dietetics, of Rockville, Maryland, for contributing the Healthful Hints.

Dr. and Mrs. Ralph Lupin, for allowing me the use of their lovely home.

M.S. Rau Antiques of Royal Street, for the use of many lovely serving pieces.

The local residents, who supported our restaurant daily and recommended us to tourists, including numerous television and movie stars.

Everyone tho contributed to compiling the data in this book.

❦ *Foreword*

In her creative manner, the author has presented in this book a work of culinary and literary art. It contains a comprehensive collection of recipes, their history and the practical steps for their production that will delight both the enchanted newcomer and the long-term devotee of Louisiana cuisine.

It is all here, from every section of the state (and from some nearby states as well) to satisfy all palates for all occasions, and some of the curiosity surrounding erstwhile guarded family and exclusive restaurant recipes.

In compiling the recipes for this volume, Miss Ruby has included those that reflect the potpourri of international influences upon the preparation of Louisiana's prolific agricultural products and of the fish, seafood and wildlife that abound in our rivers and bayous, our lakes and bays, and in the Gulf of Mexico.

In addition, she has invited her family members and friends into the reader's kitchen to add to his or her enjoyment, to stir nostalgic memories and to guarantee success.

Bon Appetit!

Lindy (Mrs. Hale) Boggs

❦ Introduction

Over the years, Miss Ruby has collected recipes from friends who are very fine cooks. Many of these recipes are served in her restaurant in New Orleans, *Miss Ruby's*, and are great favorites with her customers. All of the recipes in this book were tested in Miss Ruby's kitchen, and are proven to be excellent.

Miss Jean, Miss Ruby's eldest daughter, created all of the wonderful desserts, and the chicken and dumplings that Miss Ruby's customers enjoy. It all started when Miss Jean and her sister Martha were visiting their mom in 1984, about six months after *Miss Ruby's* opened. Miss Jean realized that Miss Ruby needed some help at the restaurant, so she arranged for an extra two weeks of vacation. Five years later, Miss Jean is still baking cakes, running the lunch business, and helping Miss Ruby manage the restaurant. This just may go on record as the longest, most strenuous vacation in recent history.

Some of the recipes in Miss Ruby's cookbook were given to her by her close friend Linda Lake Young, granddaughter of the great oil man, Pete Lake, who was the partner of the famous H.L. Hunt. Linda and her husband, Robert Earl Young, majority shareholder of several Oklahoma banks, are frequent guests at Miss Ruby's French Quarter home. On these occasions, Miss Ruby, Linda and Robert enjoy visiting and exchanging recipes while they cook in Miss Ruby's kitchen. Then, they relax by the fountain under the banana trees in the courtyard garden and enjoy the fruits of their labors. One of Miss Ruby's favorite dishes from these cooking parties is Linda's Oklahoma Chili, which is so good that they not only eat it for supper but, also, for breakfast the next morning. This "Oakie" chili is a great favorite with Miss Ruby's customers.

Several of the recipes were contributed by Miss Ruby's very dear friend Lupita Sarria. Lupita and her husband, Nick Sarria, live in Seattle, Washington, where Nick is an executive with the Boeing Co. Miss Ruby says that a trip to Seattle isn't complete without dinner in the Sarria home. Lupita is of French Basque origin. Her father was from French Basque country, an area that lies in both France and Spain, and is divided by the Pyrenees mountains. The cooking of the region reflects both French and Spanish influences. The Spanish contributions to French Basque cuisine are pimientos, red and green chile peppers, and garlic, while the preparation of the food shows the finesse of French cuisine. Lupita's father came to the United States as a young man and became a self-taught chef. He passed many of his secrets on to his daughter who has in turn shared them with Miss Ruby for this book.

Several of the recipes in the book were contributed by Joann Suckow, one of the most popular models in New Orleans and a very accomplished chef. During her modeling career, she has been an active runway model and also has represented all the major cosmetic houses. Joann lives in Kenner, Louisiana, with her husband, Bob, and two sons, David and Mark. Her recipes have been featured in many of Louisiana's food publications and she has been very active in New Orleans food trade shows.

🍎 Miss Ruby's Biography

I was born on a ranch in northern Alabama, the eighth of nine children. I learned responsibility at an early age, as each of us had daily chores we performed to help with the running of the house and the farm. We also had plenty of playtime. My favorite thing to do was to ride our horses; I loved galloping through my father's fields because it made me feel as free as a bird.

I'll never forget the year my brother Harvey bought the racehorse. Every year when the cotton was harvested, my father, Will Beard, gave each of the boys the income from a certain number of acres as payment for his work. Harvey wanted a racehorse so badly that he couldn't stand it, and when he got his money that year he went out and spent every dime on this really beautiful filly named Dixie. He never raced her professionally, but all us kids who could ride well would get on her and go like the wind. I remember one day when my cousin Flora was visiting; I saddled Dixie and the two of us went for a ride. Flora climbed up behind me, and off we went. Flora couldn't ride very well, and her balance was off, so I pulled on the reins to make Dixie slow down. Instead, Dixie grabbed the bit and took off across a turnip field. Well, Flora squeezed me so hard that I thought I was going to fall off. I kept pulling on Dixie's mouth as hard as I could, but she only ran faster. We must have crossed that field in less than a minute. There were woods at the end of it, and fortunately, Dixie decided to stop. Flora slipped off and fell on the ground like a sack of potatoes, and I started laughing so hard that I couldn't breathe. Flora walked back to the house; she never would get on Dixie again.

Dad never paid the girls in our family for our chores, so I made my first money working for some neighbors. The first time I was paid, I went down to the general store and bought an elegant hat. When I got home, the whole family laughed at me, because it was a woman's hat and too sophisticated for a little girl, but that didn't bother me. That was the beginning of my hat collection, something I've been famous for over the years.

My family was not wealthy, but my parents were warm and caring, and I never felt that anything was lacking. The farm produced almost all the food needed to feed our big family, and I was accustomed to having the freshest meat and vegetables. The ham, bacon, beef and chicken, as well as all of the vegetables, were grown on the ranch. Aunt Carrie, my black mammy, and her husband, Uncle Jake, did all of the cooking, and my earliest experiments in the kitchen were under Aunt Carrie's supervision.

One day when I was about eleven, I remember watching a delivery of fertilizer being unloaded. I was sitting on one of the farm wagons, absentmindedly watching the city boys heaving down the bags, when a thought struck me. The boys were from somewhere big and exciting, a place foreign to me. It was then that I made a decision. I promised myself that some day, when I was older, I would leave the ranch. One day, I was going to live in the big city and do exciting things.

And I did just that. I married the first time at a young age, and I had five children. For a number of years, my life was devoted to raising my family with the same principles that my parents had taught me. My husband and I owned a corner grocery, and all the kids took turns helping in the store. This was one way they learned responsibility. When my oldest son, Boyd, was six, he would stand on a Coke box to reach the cash register. He always made perfect change. Though this marriage did not last, I have many fond memories from that time.

My second husband, Clinton Wilkinson, was an engineering executive with the Boeing Company. Clint became the chief engineer of the Apollo S.I.C., the Big Booster, which was assembled at the Michoud plant in New Orleans. During this period, I joined the Krewe of Iris, which is a ladies' Mardi Gras organization. The second year I was in New Orleans, I was asked to be the Queen at the annual Mardi Gras ball. I was so surprised, and I told the ladies I wanted to consult Clint, because I knew it was a large responsibility. Clint said, "Ruby, you've always been a bright-lights kid. You know you'll enjoy yourself, so you go right ahead." I must admit I had a wonderful time, though the honor did include much time and effort on my part.

It was the same year the tragic accident occurred at Cape Kennedy, when the three astronauts died. Boeing was chosen as the consulting firm to research the incident to prevent future accidents of this nature. Boeing selected Clint to be its consultant to the NASA program in Washington, D.C. So the two of us packed up and moved to the nation's capitol. Clint supervised all phases of the Apollo program for two years; from the time the switch was pulled until splashdown, Clint was responsible for the program that put man on the moon. These years were trying, tense times for us, because Clint worked hard under a lot of pressure. I stood behind him as his wife, confidant and advisor, and Clint often said that, without my support, he would never have made it through those two years.

After our time in Washington, we moved to Seattle where Clint continued to work for the Boeing Co. I enjoyed the Pacific Northwest, but I missed New Orleans. Before Clint died, he urged me to return to New Orleans.

Early in 1984, I opened a small catering business. All the years Clint and I had spent entertaining in New Orleans, Washington, D.C., and Seattle provided me with all the experience I needed to make a catering business successful. I had been open just one month when my customers and friends began encouraging me to start a restaurant. The World's Fair was just about to open, and I decided a restaurant might be lucrative. So, *Miss Ruby's Restaurant* opened in May of 1984 in a tiny location in an old warehouse. The restaurant became very successful, and I believe it was largely due to the freshness of the food, the culinary abilities of our chefs, and the fact that the restaurant staff really enjoyed working together. Over the years, we have built up a sizable local following — people who enjoy our food and our company enough to eat with us several times a week. It was also gratifying that so many of the tourists who have eaten at my restaurant were sent by New Orleanians who loved our food.

Now the time has come to share those recipes my customers have enjoyed over the years. I have never been a cook who kept her recipes secret, because I believe sharing is so important. Recipes shared with others live forever; those that are kept secret always die. So here it is — a collection of my favorite recipes. I hope you will enjoy them.

I look forward to meeting you,

Miss Ruby

❦ About New Orleans

New Orleans has long held a reputation for great cuisine, and this had daunted some visitors who hesitate to prepare the local food because they think that it is rich, expensive and difficult to cook. It comes as a surprise that many of the favorite dishes, such as Gumbo, Jambalaya, Shrimp Creole and Crawfish Etouffee, require only one pot and are very simple to make.

Southern Louisiana has been the biggest contributor to New Orleans' cuisine. When the first European settlers arrived in the area, they had to learn how to cook with the available ingredients. They were accustomed to cooler climates that grew entirely different produce. The Indians taught them how to cook rice, fish, crabs, crawfish and shrimp. Louisiana Gumbo is a blending of Indian and French cooking methods. The Indians taught the settlers to thicken this fish soup with ground sassafras leaves, called file (pronounced *fee-lay*). The French added the roux (pronounced *roo*), a carefully browned combination of flour and fat, which gives the gumbo its rich, dark color, serves as a thickening agent, and retards spoilage. The hot peppers that spice gumbo came from Central American indians and were introduced to Louisiana by the Spanish.

The blacks of New Orleans, who have always been among the city's best cooks, have also added to the unique quality of the local cuisine.

The cuisine developed from the available ingredients. Louisiana's warm climate produces a wealth of vegetables and fruits: tomatoes, okra, mirlitons, cushaw squash, bell peppers, garlic, onions, eggplant, broccoli, cauliflower, beans, corn, hot peppers, rice, yams, sugar cane, strawberries and a variety of other fruits. A major exception is the apple, which will not grow in the warm climate. In addition to the plentiful seafood, game plays an important part. Many dishes are prepared with duck, grouse, quail, deer, rabbits, frogs and turtles.

Often, Creole and Cajun cuisine are confused with each other. But these are entirely different kinds of cooking.

The Creoles were settlers who came directly from France and lived in New Orleans or on large plantations. The Acadians were originally from France, too, but arrived via Canada and settled in the wild swamps west and south of the city. The Acadians, or Cajuns as they came to be called, were not wealthy people. Daily existence was a constant battle. While the Cajuns were struggling on the bayous, the Creoles were living a luxurious life in New Orleans, eating nine-course meals that were often prepared by cooks who came from the "old world." Consequently, Creole cuisine is richer, relies heavily on sauces, and is more similar to French cuisine than is Cajun cooking.

❦ Fairs and Festivals

Louisiana's festivals and fairs reflect the unique foods, wild game, entertainment and livelihood of its people. For example:

The Gumbo Festival
The Sugar Cane Festival
The French Quarter Festival
The Laplace Andouille Festival
The Strawberry Festival
The International Alligator Festival
The New Orleans Jazz and Heritage Festival
The Louisiana Crawfish Festival
The Crawfish Tradeshow
The Louisiana Accordion Festival
And many, many more . . .

The fairs and festivals are an integral part of the lives of the people of Louisiana and demonstrate their hospitality and "good time" attitude. This is part of what makes Louisiana a fun state.

🍒 All About Garlic

Garlic has long been used for medicinal purposes, considered for centuries to be a "cure-all" by peasants. Even today, in the age of organ transplants and artificial hearts, garlic is used to treat various illnesses: artherosclerosis (Germany), meningitis (China), anemia (Australia), colitis (Russia), diabetes (India), hypertension (Switzerland), and arthritis and pneumonia (Japan). The benefits of this "peasant penicillin" in treating these diseases have not been substantiated, but garlic's value in adding flavor to dull and boring food is well documented.

Garlic powder is no substitute for the real thing, but the powder can be used along with fresh garlic to enhance the flavor of gumbo, red beans, stews and other dishes.

If the inconvenience of mincing garlic (smelly fingers) keeps you from using it on a regular basis, make your own instant fresh garlic to keep on hand. Here's how:

Separate an entire head of garlic into cloves and peel each clove with a sharp paring knife (or, as my chefs do, mash each clove with a mallet and the skin will come off easily). Then, mince the garlic, place it in a jar, cover with vinegar or olive oil and store in the refrigerator. One teaspoon of minced garlic is equal to one medium clove of garlic.

If you prefer to have frozen instant garlic, spread the minced garlic on an aluminum pan or sheet of foil and freeze uncovered so that the granules of garlic are separate. When frozen, scrape the garlic into a small glass jar and store in the freezer. Be sure to return the jar to the freezer promptly after each use so that the garlic will not refreeze in clumps.

❦ Seasonings

SEASONED BREAD CRUMBS

2 cups plain bread crumbs
1 teaspoon garlic powder
½ teaspoon garlic salt
1 teaspoon onion powder
1 teaspoon white pepper
1½ teaspoons black pepper
1 teaspoon Tony's creole seasoning
½ teaspoon Lawry's seasoned salt
1 cup chopped parsley
1 teaspoon Italian seasoning
5 cloves garlic, finely chopped

Mix all ingredients well and put into a tightly covered container. Refrigerate or freeze. Take out and use as needed.

Here at Miss Ruby's, we make our own plain bread crumbs by using stale French bread. We place the bread into a warm oven and leave it there until it's really dry and crispy. Then, we crush the bread as finely as possible by using a food processor. If you do not have the time or the French bread to make the bread crumbs, you may substitute plain Progresso bread crumbs.

These bread crumbs are good for pannéed veal, cube steak, or any meat requiring breading.

BLACKENED SEASONING SPICE

1 teaspoon cayenne pepper
1 teaspoon Lawry's seasoned salt
½ teaspoon garlic salt
2 teaspoons garlic powder
2 teaspoons onion powder
1 teaspoon black pepper
1 teaspoon white pepper
½ teaspoon poultry seasoning
½ teaspoon ground sage
½ teaspoon oregano
1 teaspoon Tony's creole seasoning
1 teaspoon paprika
1 teaspoon salt

Mix all ingredients until well blended (use a food processor if available).

MAKES 1½ OUNCES.

This seasoning can be used for Blackened Fish, Blackened Steak, or Blackened Chicken Breast. When cooking a blackened recipe, always use a heavy cast iron skillet heated to a very high heat. Use a small amount of margarine, but do not use any other seasoning.

This recipe alone is worth more than the price of this book!

❦ *Healthful Hints*

If you have high blood cholesterol, you can make the following changes to the recipes to decrease your fat and cholesterol intake.

A. GENERAL GUIDELINES

1. Keep total fat intake low by using less butter, oil and margarine.
2. Use low-fat ingredients whenever possible. For example, skim or low-fat milk instead of whole milk and lean cuts of meat (cuts without fat and chicken and poultry without skin and fat).
3. Look for the leanest bacon, or substitute ham or Canadian bacon.
4. Remove the skin from quail after cooking.
5. When cooking lamb, be sure to trim the fat.
6. Bake, steam and stew instead of frying.
7. Use egg whites or Egg Beaters instead of whole eggs.
8. Use vegetable oil or polyunsaturated margarine instead of vegetable shortening.
9. Cool soups and gumbos and skim the hardened fat before reheating and serving.
10. Nuts are high in fat, so cut down on quantities used.
11. All liver is high in cholesterol, so avoid it whenever possible.
12. When a recipe calls for ham, make sure it is lean and trimmed of fat.
13. Instead of braising vegetables, steam or boil them.
14. Whenever a recipe calls for butter, use margarine instead.
15. When preparing meatballs, use fewer eggs and more bread crumbs.
16. For beef stroganoff, substitute yogurt for sour cream, or use a sour cream substitute.
17. Use low-fat cheese and low-fat mayonnaise whenever these ingredients are needed.
18. Eat moderate portions.

B. SUGGESTIONS FOR SPECIFIC RECIPES

1. For Lupita's Salad (page 70), make sure the bacon is well drained, and remember avocados are high in fat. Use low-fat cheese.
2. For Potato Salad (page 69), reduce the number of eggs used or eliminate entirely.
3. In the Basic White Sauce (page 184), decrease the amount of margarine and use low-fat or skim milk.

4. For the gumbos, use lean ham, smoked turkey sausage or beef sausage.

5. In the cream soups, decrease the amount of butter or margarine used, and use low-fat evaporated milk.

C. KEEPING SALT INTAKE LOW

1. When a recipe calls for creole seasoning, we suggest trying Tony Chacheray's Salt Free Seasoning. If it is unavailable locally, write Creole Foods of Opelousas Inc., Opelousas, La. 70571, or call 1-800-551-9066. They accept Mastercard and Visa.

❦ Miss Ruby's Special Tips

FRESHNESS AND QUALITY

A major key to success in any recipe is the quality and freshness of the ingredients. A favorite part of my work day is my morning trip to the French Market to select the fruits and vegetables. Louisiana is blessed with mild winters, and, consequently, we have a wide variety of produce available year round. When we plan menus for the the week, we can normally count on having the desired vegetables available. But when the quality of a particular vegetable is not up to our standards, we change the menu.

One of the secrets to our lasagna and our meatballs is the quality of the ground beef. Like most restaurants, we buy our steaks and roasts from meat wholesalers, but the ground beef these suppliers carry has too much fat. After trying several different wholesalers, I finally started selecting roasts at the local supermarket and having the butcher grind the meat in front of me. This way, I know the ground beef is high-quality and practically free of fat.

VEGETABLES

At *Miss Ruby's*, we never overcook our vegetables. I suggest steaming vegetables until they are just tender; this way, they retain their color, flavor and nutritional value. To add flavor, mince a clove of garlic and sauté or steam it along with the vegetables.

OYSTERS

Before using oysters, pick up each of them and feel for pieces of shell and remove any you find. Nothing spoils an oyster dish like biting into a piece of shell. Another oyster tip — when using the juice from the oyster in a recipe, strain it through cheesecloth to eliminate the grit.

CRABMEAT

Before using lump or claw crabmeat, gently pick through it and remove pieces of shell, trying not to break up the lumps of crabmeat.

COOKING DRIED BEANS

Wash the beans. You can soak the beans overnight, but I suggest you cover the beans with water, bring to a boil for two minutes, remove from heat and allow to soak for an hour. This keeps the beans from souring, helps retain the vitamins, reduces the number of hard skins, and cuts down on the cooking time. I find this way preferable to the soaking method.

Add salt and seasoning only after soaking. Salt has a tendency to toughen them, and therefore increases the cooking time.

To keep beans from boiling over, add a piece of bacon fat, slab bacon or butter to the pot.

One cup of dried beans yields approximately 2 to 2¾ cups of cooked beans.

Beans are nutritionally high in protein, but lack two essential amino acids required to be a "complete" protein. When beans are combined with rice, the resulting dish provides "complete" protein.

HERBS

Fresh herbs will grow on any sunny windowsill in small pots. This way, they can be used for cooking throughout the winter when they are not readily available. When substituting dried herbs for fresh, use half the amount called for, as the flavor of dried herbs is more intense.

❧ Necessary Utensils

BASTER — A bulb baster for meats is one of those gadgets every kitchen needs. It is particularly handy for basting any meat cooked in an open pan. A bulb baster will reduce the risk of burning yourself.

BLENDER — An electric blender is the cook's best friend. A four-speed model is sufficient.

COFFEE GRINDER — A coffee grinder is wonderful. Whether you use an electric or hand-operated grinder, this is the best way to have truly flavorful coffee.

DUTCH OVEN — A Dutch oven with a lid is perfect for browning roasts or meats for stew. The heat is evenly distributed, making the Dutch oven good for simmering meats for a long period of time.

FOOD PROCESSOR — Not necessary, but certainly a wonderful time-saving device when lots of vegetables need to be chopped.

GARLIC PRESS — Keeps your hands from getting so smelly when a recipe calls for minced garlic.

JUICER — An electric juicer for freshly squeezed vegetable or fruit juice.

NONSTICK PANS — Ideal for cooking omelettes. Be sure to use a hard rubber spatula to avoid scratching the surface. I use mine for eggs only.

PEPPER MILL — There is an incredible difference between freshly ground pepper and pre-ground pepper.

TIMER — A timer has saved many a meal from being overcooked.

TONGS — Stainless steel tongs are useful for turning fried chicken and for picking up hot crabs and lobsters.

WHISK — A stainless steel wire whisk is wonderful for beating eggs or anything else that needs to be beaten lightly. Whisks are available in several sizes.

❦ Glossary and Terms

A LA CREOLE — Dishes prepared with tomatoes, green peppers and onions.

ANDOUILLE — A hard, smoked, highly seasoned creole-acadian smoked sausage, common along the lower Mississippi River.

AU JUS — Served in natural juice or meat drippings.

BISQUE — A thick cream soup containing fish, game or puréed vegetables.

BOUQUET GARNI — A small cheesecloth bag containing 1 bay leaf, ¼ teaspoon of thyme, 8 sprigs of parsley, 3 chopped green celery tops, 6 whole peppercorns and 1 slashed clove of garlic.

CAFE AU LAIT — Strong hot black coffee combined with hot milk in equal proportions.

CAFE BRULOT — Spices and other ingredients flamed in brandy and added to hot coffee.

CAJUN COOKING — The cuisine of the Acadian settlers of the bayou country. Cajun cuisine is very robust and inventive; it sprang from the necessity of "making do" with available ingredients.

CELERY — A bunch of celery means the entire celery, while a stalk of celery means a single piece from the bunch.

CHICKEN BASE — Concentrated chicken stock. It is like a paste and is used mainly for restaurant use. Chicken bouillon granules may be substituted.

CHICORY — A white root that is dried, roasted and ground and then combined with coffee for a distinctive flavor.

COCHON DE LAIT — A suckling pig roasted over a blistering hickory fire until the inside is tender and juicy and the outside as brittle as well-cooked bacon.

COMPOUND BUTTER — Made by stirring fresh herbs, garlic or piquant seasoning into unsalted butter. Adds flavor to all kinds of food. Form into a log and refrigerate. Slice thickly and place on top of hot food.

CRAWFISH (crayfish, ecrevisse) — A small freshwater crustacean related to the lobster.

CREAM — Combining two or more ingredients until the mixture is light and completely blended.

CREOLE MUSTARD — A pungent, prepared mustard made from spicy brown mustard seeds.

CREOLE VEGETABLES — Vegetables grown in Louisiana.

DOBERGE — A seven-layer cake with rich chocolate cream filling.

DREDGE — To cover completely with flour or other mixture.

DRIPPINGS — The residue left in the pan after the meat or poultry is cooked; usually includes fat.

EGG WASH — A mixture of beaten egg amd milk used for frying or sautéing.

ETOUFEE — A method of cooking shrimp or crawfish in which the shell-fish are smothered in chopped vegetables, covered and cooked over a low flame until tender.

FILE — Powdered sassafras leaves, sprinkled sparingly over gumbo as a flavoring and thickening agent.

FRENCH BREAD — A long loaf of bread, crusty on the outside and fluffy white on the inside.

GARLIC — A clove of garlic is a single toe of garlic from the head. A head of garlic is the whole head — all the cloves or toes.

GARNISH — To decorate with colorful, small foods.

HUSH PUPPIES — A cornbread mixture formed into balls and fried until crispy on the outside.

JAMBALAYA — A highly seasoned mixture of any of several combinations of seafood, meats, poultry, sausage and vegetables simmered with raw rice until the liquid is absorbed.

JULIENNE — To cut into thin, narrow strips.

KNEADED BUTTER — Beurre Manie is a thickening agent is used only at the end of cooking. Equal quantities of butter and flour are mashed together to form a paste, then slowly whisked into rapidly boiling liquid. The liquid will thicken rapidly and should be served without further boiling.

LAGNIAPPE — An old creole word for "something extra."

MIRLITON — A vegetable resembling a pale green squash.

OKRA — A green tapered pod vegetable used in gumbo or served as a vegetable.

PAIN PERDU — Lost Bread or French toast.

PINCH — Less than ⅛ of a teaspoon.

ROTEL TOMATOES — Tomatoes canned with green chiles.

ROUX — A mixture of flour and oil (or fat) cooked until very brown with a nut-like flavor and aroma. Used for thickening sauces and soups.

SAUCE PIQUANTE — A thick, sharply flavored sauce made with roux and tomatoes, seasoned with herbs and peppers, and simmered for hours.

SAUTÉ — To fry a short length of time, stirring or turning frequently in a small amount of oil (fat, butter, margarine).

SHALLOT — A bulbous herb with an onion-like flavor. In Louisiana, the term applies to the scallion or green onion tops as well as the bulb.

SMOTHER — To cook slowly in a covered pot or skillet with a little liquid added to a sautéed mixture.

STOCK — Liquid in which meat, fish, poultry or vegetables have been cooked.

TABASCO — A very hot red sauce made from ground hot peppers which are fermented and mixed with vinegar. Made in Avery Island, Louisiana.

TASSO — Cajun ham smoked and cured in cayenne pepper.

YAMS — A moist, orange-colored variety of sweet potato.

🍂 Menus

Wine recommendations in the following menu suggestions were made by Erin Ryan White, the sommelier at The Grill Room, the five-star restaurant of the world-famous Windsor Court Hotel in New Orleans.

Price Guide To Wines:
- A = Inexpensive (less than $8)
- B = Moderate (between $8 and $15)
- C = Expensive ($15 to $25)
- D = Very Expensive ($25 to $50)
- E = Luxury (more than $50)

If you find some of these wines are not readily available in your supermarket, take time to visit a wine store. Don't be afraid to ask for assistance. A carefully chosen bottle of wine will make all the difference.

EASTER DINNER

Small Fried Soft Shell Crabs

Cream of Mushroom Soup

Stuffed Leg of Lamb with Brown Butter Sauce

Zucchini and Baby Carrots

Mint Jelly in Scalloped Lemon Cups

Fresh Garden Salad

Creme de Menthe Parfait with Homemade Ice Cream

Wines:

With the appetizer and soup:
Chalone Chardonnay (C)

With the entrée:
Montelina Cabernet Sauvignon (C)

VIP DINNER

Shrimp Remoulade

Cup of Turtle Soup

Hearts of Palm Salad with Sliced Tomato

Trout Meuniere

Oven-Browned Potatoes and Steamed Broccoli

Chocolate Mousse

Wines:

With the appetizer, soup and salad:
Pouilly-Fume, Chateau du Nozet, Ladoucette (B)

With the entreée:
Grgich Hills Chardonnay (C)

❦

GARDEN BRUNCH

New Orleans Bloody Marys

Mint Juleps

Croissants

Fruit Compete

Eggs Benedict

Creole Coffee

Bananas Foster

Wine:

Bollinger Special Cuvee (B)

BIRTHDAY DINNER

Shrimp Cocktail or Oysters Joseph

Asparagus Salad

Long Island Roast Duck

Wild Rice

Braised Celery

Whole Cranberry Sauce in Scalloped Grapefruit Cups

Cheesecake with Cherry or Raspberry Sauce

Wines:

With the appetizer and salad:
La Crema Chardonnay (B)

With the entrée:
Chateauneuf-du-Pape, Chateau Beaucastel (C)

❦

LADIES' CLUB LUNCHEON

Bacon, Lettuce and Tomato Soup

Grilled Chicken and Spinach Salad

Hot French Bread

Devil's Food Cake

Wines:

Chardonnay from De Loach Vineyards (B)
or if you prefer a red,
Beaujolais, George Dubeouf (A)

CHRISTMAS DINNER

Turtle Soup

Grapefruit and Avocado Salad with Vinaigrette Dressing

Turkey with Giblet Gravy

Oyster Dressing and Cornbread Dressing

Candied Yams

String Beans or Fresh Brussels Sprouts

Cranberry Sauce

Jean's Home-Baked Rolls

Relish Tray

Sweet Potato Pie and Bread Pudding with Rum Sauce

Creole Coffee or Cafe Brulot

Wines:

With soup and salad:
Manzanilla Sherry
With the entrée:

1985 Clos Vougeout, Domaine Mongeard-Mungneret (E)
or for those watching their budgets:
Beaujolais Nouveau (A)

FOURTH OF JULY — SOUL FOOD

Cup of Chicken Sausage Gumbo

Barbecue Brisket

Baked Beans and Creole Turnip Greens

Potato Salad

French Bread

Peanut Butter Pie or Coconut Cream Pie

Wines:

Australian Shiraz from Lindeman's (B)
or Brown Brothers (A)

POOLSIDE PATIO PARTY

Cup of Minestrone Soup

Hot French Bread

Fried Catfish and French-Fried Potatoes

Cole Slaw

Miss Jean's Tartar Sauce

Hush Puppies

Iced Tea or Icy Cold Beer

Red Velvet Cake

Wines:

Sancerre-Chavignol, la Bourgoiese (well chilled)

AFTER THE THEATER SUPPER

Cup of Seafood Gumbo

Hot French Bread

Turkey Poulet

Amaretto Cake

Creole Coffee

Wines:

Graacher Himmereich Riesling Spatlese, Deinhard (A - B)

NEW YEAR'S DAY DINNER

Pork Loin Roast

White Cabbage with Butter

Black-Eyed Peas

Turnip Greens or Collard Greens

Cornmeal Muffins

Candied Yams

Bread Pudding

Wines:

The best white or red that you can afford.
Suggestions:
Montelina Chardonnay (B)
Calera Pinot Noir (B - C)

MARDI GRAS FEAST

Mason's Creamy Red Beans

Creole Sausage

Hot French Bread

Cole Slaw

Cold Beer

Coffee

King's Cake and a platter of Pralines

Wine:

Kendall Jackson Zinfandell (A - B)

"AFTER THE BALL"
or
A MARDI GRAS COCKTAIL PARTY

Caviar Pie and Toast Points

Stuffed Mushrooms

Baked Pecans

Marinated Crab Claws

Tipsy Tomatoes

Wines:

Choose the best you can afford. A few suggestions:
1982 Dom Perignon, Moet Chandon (E)
Veuve Cliquot, Yellow Label (C)
Roderer Estate (B)

Entertaining with Miss Ruby

Party After the Mardi Gras Ball

New Orleans Sunday Brunch

Oyster Poor Boy Sandwich on the Mississippi

Formal Seafood Dinner

Miss Jean's Dessert Buffet

Cafe Brulot

Picnic Under the Dueling Oak

Appetizers

❦ Miss Ruby's
Famous Shrimp Cocktail

1 head butter lettuce or Boston Bibb lettuce
2 or 3 cups medium shrimp, cooked and deveined (leave tails on)
1 cup Red Cocktail Sauce (see page 183)
1 lemon, quartered

Line a saucer-shaped champagne glass with lettuce. Place shrimp along the sides and fill the center with Red Cocktail Sauce. Serve with a piece of lemon.

SERVES 4.

This makes a very impressive appetizer for that special guest or the man in your life

❦ Stuffed Mushrooms

1 package (8 ounces) cream cheese
5 tablespoons Parmesan cheese (freshly grated)
2 packages (16 ounces each) fresh medium mushrooms
Freshly chopped parsley
¼ cup butter, melted
2 tablespoons grated Romano cheese (optional)

Mix the cream cheese with 3 tablespoons of the Parmesan cheese. Stuff the caps of the mushroom with the mixture.

Sprinkle with freshly chopped parsley and the remaining Parmesan, and Romano cheese.

Drizzle a small amount of butter over each and bake in a 350-degree oven for 10 to 15 minutes. Serve hot. You will need toothpicks and napkins!

SERVES 12 TO 15.

❦ Gwyn's Tipsy Tomatoes

3 quarts water
2 boxes (1 pint each) firm, ripe cherry tomatoes
1 cup gin or tequila
2 tablespoons salt

In a large saucepan, bring the water to a brisk boil. Place a few tomatoes in a strainer or colander and dip in the boiling water for 10 seconds (no longer). Remove immediately and drain. With the point of a sharp paring knife, remove the eye of each tomato (stem end) and slip off the skin. Try not to puncture the tomatoes; they should be smooth and beautiful. Place them in a glass bowl, cover with plastic wrap, and refrigerate until ready to use.

At party time, place the gin or tequila in a small crystal bowl beside the dish of tomatoes. Provide long toothpicks and an open salt cellar. Guests will enjoy dipping the tomatoes into the alcohol and touching them with salt. This makes an unusual and refreshing hors d'oeuvre.

SERVES 15.

❦ Whole Beef Tenderloin for Hors d'Oeuvres

1 whole beef tenderloin
6 strips bacon
1 bottle (5 ounces) A-1 Sauce
¼ pound butter
1 can (7 ounces) mushroom buttons, undrained
1 loaf French bread

Preheat oven to 400 degrees. Lay strips of bacon over the tenderloin and place on a rack in a roasting pan. Bake uncovered for 15 to 25 minutes (15 minutes for rare to 25 minutes for well-done, or use a meat thermometer).

While the meat is cooking, heat to boiling the A-1 Sauce, butter, and mushrooms with juice. Cut the bread into bite-sized pieces.

To serve, place hot meat on a garnished platter. Serve bread on a separate tray beside the chafing dish containing sauce. Slice bite-sized pieces of meat very thin, dip them in the sauce and place the desired amount on a piece of bread. Eat as small open-faced sandwiches.

SERVES 10 TO 12.

Four tenderloins will serve about 50 with double the sauce.

❦ *Caviar-Stuffed Celery*

1 bunch celery hearts
1 package (8 ounces) cream cheese, softened
2 tablespoons milk
1 tablespoon chopped chives
2 tablespoons chopped parsley
3 tablespoons caviar (we recommend red lumpfish or salmon)

Trim and wash the celery stalks. Cut them in 3-inch pieces and set aside. Place the softened cheese in a bowl and mix with the milk until smooth. Stir in the chives, parsley, and 2 tablespoons of the caviar, and spread onto the celery pieces. Cover with plastic wrap and chill well. Just before serving, garnish with additional caviar.

MAKES 14 PIECES.

This dish is quick and easy to prepare. As a professional caterer, I find it a favorite at cocktail parties. It is pretty to look at and tastes wonderful.

❦ Fried Crab Claws

2 pounds crab claws
1 cup flour
½ teaspoon Lawry's seasoned salt
½ teaspoon creole seasoning (we prefer Tony's)
½ teaspoon freshly ground black pepper
1 egg
1 cup milk
2 cups peanut oil (we prefer Louana)

If the crab claws are frozen, thaw them in the refrigerator or at room temperature. Put the flour and the seasonings in a bowl and mix. Make the "egg wash" in another bowl by beating the egg with a wire whisk and then adding the milk. Heat the oil to 375 degrees in a heavy skillet or deep fat fryer. Use enough to cover 1 pound of claws in each cooking. Be sure to use a fry basket. Dip the claws in the seasoned flour mixture, then in the egg wash, and back into the flour. Drop the battered claws into the hot oil and cook until golden-brown.

These make an excellent party dish when served with our Red Cocktail Sauce (see page 183) or Garlic Mayonnaise (see page 178).

SERVES 10 OR MORE.

❦ Angels on Horseback

1 pint select oysters, shucked
¾ pound sliced bacon
1 box wooden party toothpicks
1 bunch fresh watercress
6 slices white bread, crusts removed

Drain the oysters in a colander. Cut the bacon slices in half, wrap each oyster in one piece of bacon, and secure with a toothpick. Place the wrapped oysters on a baking sheet and broil for 2 to 3 minutes on each side or until the bacon is crisp. (Alternative method: Bake in a 400-degree oven for 5 to 7 minutes.)

To serve as an hors d'oeuvre, arrange on a platter garnished with watercress and provide additional toothpicks for guests.

To serve as an appetizer, toast and butter the bread squares, remove the toothpicks from the angels and garnish with fresh watercress.

SERVES 4 TO 6.

Devils on Horseback are pitted prunes wrapped in bacon and broiled.

❦ Sausage Cheese Balls

1 pound hot breakfast sausage
3 cups Bisquick
10 ounces sharp cheddar cheese

Leave the sausage out until it reaches room temperature. Grate the cheese. Mix all three ingredients together. Roll into small balls using a teaspoon of the mixture for each ball.

Bake at 350 degrees for 15 to 20 minutes on a cookie sheet. These freeze well.

SERVES 10 TO 12.

Great served with warm honey.

❦ Caviar Pie

6 hard-boiled eggs, peeled
1 package (8 ounces) cream cheese
1 jar (1 ounce) black caviar (we recommend sturgeon)
6 green onions, finely chopped
1 jar (4 ounces) red caviar (we recommend red lumpfish or salmon)
½ cup finely chopped parsley
8 thin slices white bread, crusts trimmed

Cut the eggs in half and remove the yolks. Chop the yolks and the whites into separate bowls and set aside. Soften the cream cheese with a little cream and spread it on a 10-inch round platter. On this cheese base, you will build the "pie."

Mound the black caviar in the center of the cheese base. Surround the caviar with circles of chopped egg yolks, green onions, red caviar, chopped egg whites, and parsley. Cover the dish loosely with plastic wrap and refrigerate until serving time. This may be prepared as much a day ahead of time.

To make toast points, cut each slice of bread into four triangles. Spread them out on a cookie sheet and bake in a 450-degree oven, turning once, until lightly toasted on both sides. Store the toast points in a tightly covered container so they will remain crisp.

SERVES 18 TO 20.

See photograph of Mardi Gras party.

❦ Cucumber Sandwiches

2 cucumbers
1½ teaspoons salt, or to taste
6 slices whole wheat bread
6 tablespoons butter, softened
3 hard-boiled eggs, sieved
12 pitted California ripe olives, thinly sliced
Sour Cream Whip
Sliced green onions

Peel the cucumbers and slice very thinly. Sprinkle cucumber slices lightly with the salt. Chill for at least 30 minutes.

Squeeze out the excess moisture from the cucumbers. Spread the butter on the bread and arrange the cucumber slices, sieved eggs, and olives on the bread. Top with Sour Cream Whip and sprinkle on the green onions. Cut each sandwich into quarters to serve.

SERVES 6.

SOUR CREAM WHIP
¾ cup sour cream
1 teaspoon lemon juice
1 teaspoon green onion, thinly sliced
½ teaspoon salt

Combine all the ingredients in a small bowl and mix well.

MAKES ¾ CUP.

Beverages

❦ Beth Ann's Confederate Punch

This recipe belonged to President James Monroe (1817-1825). He is reported to have said its one purpose was to banish all inhibitions. Beth Ann says it's nothing short of dynamite.

2 gallons green tea
4 to 6 cans (21 ounces each) pineapple
2 pounds fresh cherries (or 2 to 3 cans of pie cherries, drained)
2 gallons Santa Cruz Rum
1 gallon Hennessey Three Star Brandy
1 gallon Beefeater's Gin
1 gallon Rye Whiskey

Make the tea with 1 pound of tea and 2 gallons of cold water. Soak overnight. (To shorten this process, pour 1 gallon boiling water over the tea and let steep 5 minutes, and then add 1 gallon of cold water).

Add the pineapple and the cherries to the tea and sweeten to taste, normally 1 to 2 cups of sugar depending on the tartness of cherries. Let this stand overnight

Combine all the ingredients, cover, and allow to stand for 2 weeks (any sooner, and it's not nearly as good). This recipe makes approximately 10 gallons of punch, and may be made in a good-quality ice chest. Of course, the quantities may be reduced.

Serve well-chilled in a punch bowl with a block of ice. Beth Ann sometimes uses orange juice frozen in loaf pans instead of plain ice, or frozen 7-Up or ginger ale. For a little excitement, throw in a piece of dry ice for a really "smoking" brew.

The taste is very similar to Long Island Ice Tea.

This recipe comes from Beth Ann Bertucci's grandmother, Mattie McClary (Miss Mattie). Miss Mattie always said this was really a southern recipe, because James Monroe was from Virginia, and because it was often served under the sassafras tree.

❦ Mint Juleps

4 mint leaves
1 tablespoon sugar
1½ ounces bourbon whiskey
1 sprig of mint

Crush the mint leaves and the sugar together with a mortar and pestle to make a paste. Put the paste and the bourbon in a tall highball glass and fill with crushed ice. Stir until the glass is well-frosted on the outside. Serve garnished with a sprig of mint.

❦ Ramos Gin Fizz

½ ounce lemon juice
1 ounce simple syrup
1 egg white
2 ounces gin
1 dash orange flower water

Shake all the ingredients in a bar shaker with several lumps of ice. Strain into a tall glass and top with a splash of club soda.

❦ Our Famous Freshly Squeezed Lemonade

2 cups sugar
1 cup fresh lemon juice
Cold water to fill a 1-gallon jug

Stir all the ingredients well and refrigerate overnight. This beverage will keep up to 2 weeks if kept cold.
    Serve in a tall glass over ice and garnish with a slice of lemon.

❦ Sazarac

2 ounces rye whiskey
½ ounce simple syrup
4 dashes Paychaud bitters
Herbsaint or Pernod to coat the glass

Chill an old-fashioned bar glass and coat with Herbsaint or Pernod. Put the rye whiskey, simple syrup, and bitters in a cocktail shaker and stir. Pour into the glass and top with a twist of lemon.

This recipe was given to me by my good friend, Michael Heckler, who was my assistant at many of the parties we catered. He is now the manager of Moran's Riverside Restaurant here in New Orleans.

❦ Happy Marriage

2 cups hot chocolate, cooled
1 cup cold strong coffee
Sugar, to taste
¾ cup brandy
¾ cup whipped cream

Combine the chocolate and coffee in a mixing bowl; sweeten with sugar. Whip vigorously with a wire whisk until frothy. Stir in the brandy. Pour into two tall glasses and spoon the whipped cream on top. Serve with long spoons for stirring.

This beverage may also be served hot in mugs.

❦ Bud's Bloody Mary Mix

1 can (10 ounces) beef consommé
2 cans (32 ounces each) tomato juice or V-8 vegetable juice
1 bottle (8 ounces) clam juice
5 ounces Worcestershire sauce
3 tablespoons celery salt
2 tablespoons black pepper
Tabasco sauce, to taste

In a glass pitcher, mix all ingredients well. Fill a double old-fashioned glass with ice, add your favorite gin or vodka, and add the mix. Stir well and garnish with a tender stalk of celery. Makes a perfect Bloody Mary.

    This mix will keep well in the refrigerator for 1 week.

❦ Beth Ann's Fruity Punch

½ gallon Hawaiian punch concentrate
3 cans (15 ounces each) crushed pineapple
1 can (15 ounces each) fruit cocktail
3 bottles dry white wine, vodka, or rum
2 gallons water, boiled and cooled
1½ gallons pineapple sherbet

Chill the punch concentrate, crushed pineapple, fruit cocktail, and liquor until very cold. In a mold or tube cake pan, freeze the water to make ice rings. You may float fresh fruit or flowers in the rings before freezing. Before serving, mix all the ingredients in a punch bowl and float the ice ring and sherbet on the top.

    SERVES UP TO 100.

🍒 Chase's Essence Bloody Mary Mix

2 teaspoons salt
1 teaspoon celery salt
½ teaspoon black pepper
½ teaspoon sugar
2 tablespoons lime juice, scant
2 tablespoons Worcestershire sauce
½ scant tablespoon Tabasco sauce

Mix all ingredients in a covered jar and refrigerate. When ready to use, pour the desired amount of vodka or gin in a glass. Add 1 teaspoon of Chase's Essence, ice, and tomato juice or V-8 cocktail. Perfect every time!

🍒 Creole Coffee

4 cups boiling water
1 cup dark roast chicory coffee

Pour first about 10 tablespoons of boiling water on the coffee grounds to settle them. Wait about 5 minutes and pour a little more water and allow it to drip slowly through the grounds. Continue to pour water until all is used but never add more until the grounds have ceased to puff or bubble.

Cafe au Lait is made by simultaneously pouring hot milk or cream and hot coffee into a cup in order to get about a 50-50 mixture.

❦ Cafe Brulot

4 ounces Cognac
2 ounces Cointreau
2 ounces Grand Marnier
¼ cup whole cloves
2 tablespoons sugar
1 orange
1 lemon
2 cinnamon sticks
12 ounces brewed coffee

UTENSILS
20-ounce chafing dish
1 stand with heat
4 Brulot cups
1 ladle with screen
1 fork
1 paring knife

In the chafing dish, combine the Cognac, Cointreau, Grand Marnier, 1 tablespoon whole cloves, the cinnamon sticks broken into thirds, and 2 tablespoons sugar. Bring this mixture slowly to a boil.

While this mixture is heating, peel the lemon and orange without breaking the peel. Add the lemon and its peel to the mixture. Then, take the extended orange peel and pierce it with whole cloves at 2-inch intervals. With the fork, take the orange and hold it about 2 feet above the chafing dish and extend the peel to the top of the dish. Light the mixture. Fill the ladle half full of the lighted mixture and gradually pour over the whole orange so the mixture slowly flows down the extended orange peel. Repeat this procedure 2 or 3 times for show. Add the coffee to the mixture to extinguish the flames. Add the orange to the mixture. Let sit 2 minutes. Ladle into the Brulot cups and serve.

> *This recipe was given to me by my good friend Jim Kellet, maitre d' of the famous Versailles Restaurant on St. Charles Avenue in New Orleans.*
>
> *See photograph.*

❦ Hot Buttered Rum

2 ounces light rum
Juice of 1 small lemon
1 small strip of lemon peel
1½ teaspoons brown sugar
1½ teaspoons butter

Place a long spoon in a tall glass. Pour the rum into the glass. Add the lemon juice and lemon peel. Pour enough boiling water into the glass over the handle of the spoon to fill the glass. Stir in the brown sugar, add the butter, and stir until the butter is melted. Garnish with a slice of lemon and additional lemon peel.

> *Use the best rum for this drink. It is an especially welcome treat in chilly weather.*

❦ Pink Lady

1 tablespoon crushed ice
Juice of ⅓ lemon, strained
Juice of 1 lime, strained
Juice of 1 chilled orange, strained
2 tablespoons confectioner's sugar
1 egg yolk
Chilled soda water

In a cocktail shaker, combine the crushed ice, fruit juices, sugar, and egg yolk. Cover and shake vigorously. Strain into a tall, thin, stemmed glass and fill the glass with soda water. Garnish with a cherry and a long thin shred of orange peel, or top with sherbet or ice milk.

> *The look of this drink is very important.*

> *If you like, you may add cranberry juice, apple juice, or ginger ale.*

Soups and Gumbos

❦ Linda's Tortilla Soup

4 to 6 chicken breasts, skinned and boned
1 fresh lime
1 teaspoon garlic salt
1 teaspoon onion powder
1 teaspoon freshly ground black pepper
6 cans (14½ ounces each) chicken broth
2 cans (6 ounces each) tomato sauce
3 large fresh tomatoes, diced
2 bunches green onions, tops and bottoms chopped
Cayenne pepper, to taste
2 ripe avocados, diced
½ cup cheddar cheese, grated
2 corn tortillas, cut in 1-by-2-inch strips

Place the chicken breasts in a baking dish and sprinkle with the lime juice, garlic salt, onion powder, and black pepper. (This dish is excellent when cooked on an outdoor grill.) Bake or broil until done. Cut the chicken into strips and set aside.

Meanwhile, put the chicken broth in a soup pot and add the tomato sauce, fresh tomatoes, green onions, and cayenne pepper. Simmer until the onions are tender, then add the chicken pieces, and heat thoroughly.

Serve in bowls topped with diced avocados, grated cheddar cheese, and tortilla chips. Serve additional tortilla chips on the side.

Linda buys corn tortillas at the grocery store. While the soup is cooking, she cuts them in strips, sprinkles them with salt, fries them in peanut oil, and drains them on paper towels.

SERVES 6 TO 8.

This is indeed a delicious, healthy one-dish meal. Linda says this is her husband's favorite. I'm sure it will please the man in your life, too. Any leftovers are good the next day.

❦ Cream of Chicken Soup

1 chicken (3½ pounds)
Salt and pepper, to taste
1 stick butter or margarine
½ cup flour
1 tablespoons chicken base or bouillon cubes or granules
1 quart milk
1 can (10 ounces) evaporated milk
1 teaspoon white pepper
2 cups chicken stock

Boil the chicken in a large pot with salt and pepper to taste. Cook until tender (about 1½ hours). Remove the chicken from the stock, set stock aside, and allow chicken to cool. Remove the chicken from the bones and chop the meat into cubes.

Melt the butter or margarine over a medium heat in a large pot and add flour to make a roux. Add the chicken base, milk, evaporated milk, white pepper, and chicken stock. Using a wire whisk, beat constantly until creamy and smooth. Add chopped chicken and cook 5 minutes.

SERVES 6 TO 8.

❦ Bacon, Lettuce, and Tomato Soup

1 pound bacon
2 tomatoes, finely chopped
½ head iceberg lettuce, shredded
½ cup bacon drippings
½ cup flour
1 quart milk
1 can (10 ounces) evaporated milk
4 green onions, chopped
1 tablespoon chicken base or chicken bouillon cubes
½ teaspoon white pepper
Dash cayenne pepper

Fry bacon, drain, and crumble. Chop tomatoes, shred lettuce and set aside.

Use bacon drippings and flour to make a roux. Cook over medium heat until roux is an even, medium brown (see Roux, page 181). Add milk, evaporated milk, green onions, chicken base, white pepper, and cayenne pepper. Cook until thick and creamy. Stir constantly with a wire whisk.

Serve in open bowls and top with crumbled bacon, chopped tomatoes, and shredded lettuce.

SERVES 8.

Delicious!

❦ *Cream of Mushroom Soup*

4 green onions, chopped
3 tablespoons butter
1 pound fresh mushrooms, sliced
4 cups chicken stock
1 cup cream or evaporated milk
Salt and pepper, to taste
Dash white pepper
Dash cayenne pepper

Sauté onions in butter in a large pot. Add the mushrooms and continue to sauté for 5 minutes more. Add the chicken stock and bring to a boil. Simmer for 30 minutes. Pour mixture into a blender or food processor and blend until smooth. Return soup to pot and add cream, salt, white pepper, and cayenne pepper. Reheat.

Serve in bowls, top with a dash of cayenne, and garnish with a few fresh mushroom slices.

SERVES 6.

❦ Sherried Turtle Soup

4 pounds turtle meat
2 gallons water
12 hard-boiled eggs
½ pound butter or margarine
3 onions, finely chopped
½ bunch celery, finely chopped
3 bell peppers, finely chopped
6 cloves garlic, minced
1 teaspoon red pepper
1½ teaspoons Lawry's seasoned salt
1 teaspoon thyme
1 teaspoon black pepper
4 bay leaves
1 cup Worcestershire sauce (we prefer Lea & Perrin's)
1 can (9 ounces) tomato purée
1 can (12 ounces) whole tomatoes, chopped
1 cup Dry Sac Sherry or any good sherry
1 cup peanut oil (we prefer Louana)
2 cups flour
2 large lemons, juiced

In a large saucepan, place the turtle meat in 1 gallon of water and boil over medium heat for 1 hour. Remove the meat and set aside to cool. Save the stock. Chop the turtle meat very finely but leave some small chunks. Chop the boiled eggs and set aside. In a large heavy pot (4-gallon size), melt the butter or margarine and add the onion, celery, bell pepper, and minced garlic. Sauté for 15 minutes before adding the turtle meat and all of the seasonings. Continue cooking, and add the tomato purée and the whole tomatoes. Now add the turtle meat stock and 1 gallon of water and bring to a boil. Add the chopped eggs and sherry, and continue to cook for 1 to 2 hours with the lid on.

While the soup is cooking, make a cream-colored roux using the peanut oil and flour. Cook this roux just long enough to cook the flour but do not brown. When the soup is almost done, add the roux to the pot, stirring constantly. Cook a few minutes to thicken before adding the lemon juice. Cook about 10 to 15 minutes more and remove from the heat.

As an appetizer, serve approximately 1 cup in a soup bowl topped with a thin slice of lemon and an additional dash of sherry.

Turtle Soup is an old New Orleans favorite and, like many Creole dishes, it originated because the major ingredient was readily available. Diamondback terrapin and snapping turtles are trapped in the marshes and brought into New Orleans where they are turned into a mouth-watering soup, just as they have been for more than 200 years.

Turtle Soup is on most New Orleans menus. It makes a very elegant first course at any dinner. Now you can enjoy Turtle Soup without coming to New Orleans because the meat can be bought frozen. I buy mine from Battestilla's Seafood, which ships anywhere.

To break this recipe down to household size, I had a special cooking session with one of our famous chefs. In the restaurant, we normally cook 20 to 40 gallons at a time. This freezes well for up to 6 months.

❦ Cream of Potato Soup

8 to 10 medium potatoes, peeled and cubed
1 large onion, chopped
Garlic salt, to taste
salt and pepper to taste
¼ cup butter or margarine
1 can (12 ounces) evaporated milk

Boil potatoes and onion until tender. Add seasonings, butter, and milk to the potato water and heat through.

SERVES 6 TO 8.

❦ Onion Soup

8 tablespoons butter or margarine
2 pounds white onions, thinly sliced
3 tablespoons flour
¼ teaspoon Tony's creole seasoning
Salt and freshly ground black pepper, to taste
8 cups beef stock
5 slices bread, cut in 1-inch cubes
Garlic butter (¼ cup melted margarine and ½ teaspoon garlic powder)
Parmesan cheese, freshly grated

In a 6-quart saucepan, melt the butter and stir in sliced onions. Cook over low heat about 25 minutes or until onions are golden brown. Sprinkle flour over the onions and cook, stirring 2 or 3 minutes.

Remove from heat. Add Tony's seasoning, salt, pepper, and beef stock. Stir well. Return to heat and cook slowly for 30 to 40 minutes.

Meanwhile, place bread cubes on cookie sheet. Bake at 350 degrees for 15 minutes. With a pastry brush, lightly coat the bread with garlic butter and return to oven for 5 minutes.

Just before serving, pour soup into individual bowls. Top with bread cubes and sprinkle heavily with Parmesan cheese.

SERVES 8.

❦ *Minestrone*

½ cup dried lima beans
¼ pound salt pork
Salt and freshly ground black pepper, to taste
1 onion, minced
1 clove garlic, minced
½ teaspoon thyme
2 tablespoons olive oil
5 cups beef broth or consommé
2 cups water
2 carrots, sliced
2 stalks celery, sliced
2 potatoes, cubed
¼ small head cabbage, shredded
4 tomatoes, peeled and cut up
1 cup elbow macaroni
¼ cup Parmesan cheese, freshly grated

Wash lima beans well and soak overnight in cold water.

In the morning, dice the salt pork and sauté in a heavy pot until brown. Drain the beans and add them to the pork. Cover with water and season with salt and pepper. Bring to a boil. Reduce heat and simmer 2 hours.

While the beans are cooking, prepare the vegetables. In a large pot, sauté the onion, garlic, and thyme in olive oil until tender. Add beef broth, water, carrots, celery, potatoes, cabbage, and tomatoes. Bring to a boil, reduce heat, and simmer for 1 hour.

Meanwhile, cook the elbow macaroni until tender, rinse, and drain. Add macaroni and lima beans to the soup.

Serve in open bowls topped with Parmesan cheese.

SERVES 6 TO 8.

❦ Oyster Stew

½ cup butter
5 green onions, finely chopped
1 stalk celery, chopped
1 small clove garlic, minced
⅛ teaspoon cayenne pepper
⅛ teaspoon thyme leaves, crushed
¼ cup chopped parsley
Salt and freshly ground pepper, to taste
3 tablespoons flour
24 oysters (reserve liquor)
2 cups milk
2 cups cream or evaporated milk

In a large heavy saucepan, melt butter. Add green onions, celery, and garlic. Sauté 10 minutes or until soft. Add cayenne pepper, thyme, parsley, salt, and pepper. Continue cooking for 5 minutes. Add the flour, stirring constantly until blended. Add oysters, liquor from oysters, milk, and cream. Stir gently until thoroughly heated.

SERVES 6.

Make sure you remove all pieces of shells from the oysters, and strain the oyster liquor through cheesecloth to remove all fine pieces.

❦ Beef Vegetable Soup

2 pounds chuck, cut in cubes or 2 pounds beef brisket, cut in cubes
2 gallons water
1 can (16 ounces) tomatoes
4 to 5 carrots, diced
1 pound green beans, cut in 1-inch pieces
⅓ cup fresh parsley, minced
2 cups celery, coarsely chopped
2 cups cabbage, shredded
2 large onions, chopped
2 cups corn
2 cups potatoes, diced
1 tablespoon salt, or to taste
1 tablespoon black pepper
1 package (8 ounces) vermicelli pasta, broken into short pieces

Put chuck or brisket in a large pot with water. Add tomatoes and boil over medium heat for about 2 hours.

Meanwhile, chop and prepare vegetables. Add all other ingredients and cook until vegetables and meat are tender. Add vermicelli last. If more liquid is needed, add beef broth or water.

You may substitute a 1-pound bag of mixed vegetables for the corn and beans.

SERVES 8 TO 10.

This recipe makes wonderful leftovers and also freezes well.

❦ Chef Mason's
Cream of Broccoli Soup

1 whole large bunch of broccoli
1 teaspoon salt, or to taste
⅓ cup cooking oil
6 to 7 heaping tablespoons flour
¼ teaspoon yellow food color (optional)
2 tablespoons. chicken base or chicken bouillon granules
½ teaspoon Ac'cent (monosodium glutamate)
1 teaspoon white pepper
2 cans (12 ounces) evaporated milk
Dash cayenne pepper

Cut broccoli into large chunks. Do not discard stems. In a large pot, parboil broccoli with salt in 2½ quarts of water until tender. Set aside. Remove the broccoli from the water, discard stems, and process broccoli in a food processor or chop very finely by hand. Reserve the water in which the the broccoli was boiled. This will be the base for the soup.

In another large pot, make a roux with the flour and cooking oil (see Roux, page 181). *Do not* brown the roux; simply cook until a light creamy color is achieved.

Add the broccoli water to the roux while stirring briskly with a whisk. Add broccoli, chicken base, Ac'cent, food color, and white pepper. Bring to a boil over medium heat, and boil for 3 to 5 minutes. Lower heat and stir in evaporated milk and cayenne pepper. Cook slowly for 15 minutes.

SERVES 8.

❦ *Oxtail Soup*

3 pounds oxtails
1 gallon water
Salt and freshly ground black pepper to taste
2 large onions, chopped
7 stalks celery, chopped, or 1 bunch
3 cans (16 ounces each) whole tomatoes
1 can (8 ounces) tomato sauce
2 pounds frozen mixed vegetables
2 tablespoons beef bouillon granules
2 tablespoons chicken base or bouillon granules
1 teaspoon white pepper
3 large red potatoes, diced
4 ounces egg noodles

Boil the oxtails in the water for 1½ hours or until tender. Add all the remaining ingredients, except the potatoes and noodles, and simmer over low heat for 1 to 2 hours more. Add the potatoes and noodles about 15 minutes before the soup is done. Skim off the fat and serve.

MAKES ABOUT 2 GALLONS.

This soup freezes well or keeps in the refrigerator for 4 days.

🍒 Lamplighter Club
Seafood & Sausage Gumbo

The Lamplighter Club was a membership club on the top of the Rault Center on Gravier Street in New Orleans. The club accepted men, women, and out-of-town businesspeople as members and, though it was not a petroleum club, many of its members were in the oil industry. I was a member in the 1960s, and one day when I was having lunch there, I ordered the gumbo. I was so impressed with the flavor that I went back to the kitchen to compliment the chef, and he gave me the recipe. Miss Ruby's has served the Lamplighter Gumbo to guests and customers over the years. Since the club closed during the oil recession in the 1980s, this is probably one of the few Lamplighter recipes to survive.

4 bell peppers, finely chopped
2 bunches green onions, finely chopped
1 stalk celery, finely chopped
2 large yellow onions, finely chopped
1 bunch fresh parsley, finely chopped
1 pound butter or margarine
4 pounds hot smoked sausage, thinly sliced
2½ cups cooking oil
1 can (10 ounces) Italian or Rotel tomatoes, seasoned with jalapeño peppers
4 or 5 bay leaves
3 pounds cut okra
1¼ cups flour
2 tablespoons monosodium glutamate (optional)
1 tablespoon black pepper
½ teaspoon white pepper
1 tablespoon cayenne pepper
1 tablespoon crushed red pepper
1 teaspoon garlic powder
1 teaspoon creole seasoning (we recommend Tony Chachere's)
1 teaspoon Lawry's seasoned salt
1 teaspoon thyme
¼ cup Louisiana hot sauce (optional)
1 gallon chicken stock or 1 gallon water with 2 tablespoons chicken base
    or chicken-flavored bouillon cubes or granules by Knorr
5 pounds gumbo crabs, cleaned and broken apart

1¼ cups flour
4 pounds small shrimp, peeled and deveined
1 pound crabmeat (claw or white)

Sauté bell peppers, green onions, celery, yellow onions, and parsley in butter or margarine. In another skillet, sauté sliced sausage in ½ cup cooking oil, and add to vegetables along with the can of tomatoes and the bay leaves. Simmer over low heat while sautéing okra in ½ cup cooking oil (you may use the same skillet that you used for the sausage). Now add okra, all additional seasonings, chicken stock, and gumbo crabs to the pot, and cook over low heat for about an hour.

Make a roux using 1½ cups cooking oil and flour. Remember, the darker the roux, the darker the gumbo. (See Roux, page 181.)

When gumbo is done, add roux and simmer slowly to thicken to desired consistency. Add shrimp and crabmeat at the very last, and cook briefly until shrimp is done.

Serve over rice.

SERVES 10 TO 15.

The gumbo makes a pretty serving by forming a mound, using ½ cup of rice lightly pressed into a small cup and turned into the center of a large soup bowl with the gumbo ladled around it. Serve with a crispy green salad and hot French bread.

❦ Cajun Chicken and Andouille Sausage Gumbo

1 fryer (3 to 4 pounds), cut up, or drummettes (chicken wing sections)
1½ teaspoons garlic powder
2 teaspoons cayenne pepper
1 teaspoons black pepper
1 teaspoons white pepper
1 teaspoons Lawry's seasoned salt
1 cup onions, finely chopped
1 cup green onions, chopped
1 cup bell peppers, finely chopped
1 cup parsley, chopped
1 cup celery, chopped
1½ cups flour
½ teaspoon salt
Cooking oil
1½ pounds Andouille sausage (any good smoked sausage may be substituted)
4 cloves garlic, minced
1 can (10 ounces) Rotel tomatoes
8 cups Basic Chicken Stock (see page 187)
Cooked rice

Remove excess fat from the chicken pieces. Mix 1 teaspoon of the garlic powder, peppers (reserve ½ teaspoon cayenne pepper for shaking), and Lawry's seasoned salt in a small bowl. Rub a generous amount of the mixed spices on both sides of the chicken. Make sure all pieces are coated. Let stand at room temperature for 30 minutes.

Meanwhile, combine the onion, green onion, bell pepper, parsley, and celery, and set aside.

Reserve ½ cup of the flour. Combine the rest of the flour, the salt, ½ teaspoon of the garlic powder, and ½ teaspoon of the cayenne pepper in a plastic bag. Add the chicken pieces and shake until well-coated.

In a large, heavy skillet heat 1 to 2 inches of oil until very hot (375 to 400 degrees). Fry the chicken until the meat is cooked and browned on both sides (about 8 minutes per side). Drain on a paper towel. Pour hot oil into a measuring cup, leaving all scraps in the bottom of the pan. Scrape the pan with a whisk to loosen any stuck particles. Return ½ cup of the hot oil to the pan and place over high heat.

Stir in ½ cup of the flour. Continue stirring until the flour turns dark brown to make roux (about 4 minutes). Be careful not to scorch the flour or splash your hands. Remove from heat.

Add the vegetable mixture and stir constantly to prevent the roux from becoming darker. Lower the heat and cook until vegetables are tender, about 5 minutes. Meanwhile, place the stock in a 6-quart pot or Dutch oven and bring to a boil. Add the roux mixture to the boiling stock, stirring until dissolved after each addition. Return to a boil. Stir and scrape the bottom of the pan often. Reduce to a simmer, add the sausage, garlic, and chicken. Cook uncovered for about 45 minutes. Adjust seasonings. Serve immediately.

To serve as a main course, mound ¼ cup rice in the center of each soup bowl, and ladle gumbo around rice. For an appetizer, place 1 tablespoon rice in a cup and ladle gumbo on top.

SERVES 8 AS A MAIN DISH OR 10 AS AN APPETIZER.

❦ Louisiana Seafood and Sausage Gumbo

½ cup cooking oil
1 cup onions, chopped
1 cup celery, chopped
1 cup bell pepper, chopped
1 cup fresh parsley, chopped
1 cup green onions, thinly sliced
6 cloves garlic, minced

Prepare above ingredients and set aside.

SEASONINGS
½ teaspoon Italian seasoning
½ teaspoon basil leaves
½ teaspoon poultry seasoning (optional)
1 teaspoon cayenne pepper
½ teaspoon sage
½ teaspoon oregano
1 teaspoon gumbo file
½ teaspoon garlic salt
½ teaspoon white pepper
½ teaspoon black pepper
1 teaspoon onion powder (optional)
1 teaspoon garlic powder
2 teaspoons chicken base or salt

Mix all seasonings in a bowl and set aside.

6 medium gumbo crabs (well-cleaned)
3 cups okra, sliced
¼ cup cooking oil
1 can Rotel tomatoes, seasoned with jalapeño peppers, mashed
1 cup fresh whole tomatoes
½ pound Andouille sausage (any good smoked sausage may be
    substituted)
1 gallon chicken stock

1 pound shrimp, peeled and deveined
1 cup crabmeat (lump or claw)
1 pint oysters (optional)

First, make the Roux (see page 181).

Put ½ cup of cooking oil in a large gumbo pot. Add all chopped vegetables and sauté until tender. Then, add all seasonings and gumbo crabs. While this is cooking, fry okra in ¼ cup of cooking oil until slightly done (this prevents okra from being stringy). Add to gumbo pot along with canned tomatoes, fresh tomatoes, sausage, and chicken stock. Cook slowly for 30 minutes.

Add shrimp, crabmeat, and oysters. Cook only about 5 to 10 minutes after adding seafood.

Serve over rice with hot French bread and a green salad.

SERVES 8.

A truly great meal!

Salads

❦ Potato Salad

8 potatoes, diced
6 hard-boiled eggs
½ cup sweet pickle relish
1 medium onion, finely chopped
½ cup mayonnaise
1½ teaspoons prepared yellow mustard
¼ teaspoon season salt (we prefer Tony's)
Salt and pepper, to taste

Dice the potatoes; then, boil until tender. Drain and allow to cool. Chop eggs. Add all ingredients together in a large mixing bowl, and mix well. Refrigerate.

SERVES 8.

Potato Salad will keep in the refrigerator for a week or longer.

❦ Linda's Famous Coleslaw

1 large head cabbage, coarsely chopped
2 bunches green onions, sliced in 1-inch pieces
1 bunch carrots, thinly sliced or julienned
2 green bell peppers, coarsely chopped or cut in slivers
1½ lemons, juiced
Salt and freshly ground black pepper, to taste
½ cup mayonnaise (we prefer Kraft Real Mayonnaise)

Prepare the vegetables and mix all the ingredients together in a wooden or glass salad bowl. Refrigerate for several hours.

SERVES 8.

The secret of this recipe is using a lot of lemon and chopping the vegetables coarsely. Serve with deep-fried fresh fish and French fries.

❦ Lupita's Salad Supreme

½ cup virgin olive oil
3 medium cloves garlic, minced
¼ teaspoon garlic powder
¼ teaspoon salt, or to taste
½ teaspoon freshly ground black pepper
½ teaspoon oregano
½ pound bacon, crisply fried and crumbled
3 large fresh tomatoes, cut into large chunks or wedges
1 bunch green onions
2 large avocados, cut into large chunks
1 large head Romaine lettuce
1 lemon
Freshly ground Parmesan cheese (approximately ¼ cup)

In a large salad bowl, mix together olive oil, garlic, garlic powder, salt, pepper, and oregano. Add crumbled bacon and blend well. Add tomatoes and green onions, and mix. Add avocado and mix again. Add lettuce, broken by hand into large bite-sized pieces, and toss well; let sit at room temperature. Taste for seasoning. Squeeze the lemon over the salad, and toss again. Sprinkle with freshly ground Parmesan cheese and serve.

SERVES 6 TO 8.

❦ Our Famous West Indies Salad

1 medium onion, finely chopped
1 pound fresh lump crabmeat
Freshly ground pepper, to taste
¼ teaspoon Tony's creole seasoning
4 ounces Crisco oil
3 ounces cider vinegar
4 ounces ice water
Fresh lettuce

Divide chopped onion in half, and spread half over the bottom of a large mixing bowl. Separate crabmeat lumps and place on top of onion in the bowl. Then, spread the rest of the onion on top of the crabmeat. Add pepper and creole seasoning. Over all of this, pour the oil, next the vinegar, and finally the ice water. Cover and place in refrigerator to marinate 2 to 12 hours.

When ready to serve, toss lightly but do not stir. Serve on a bed of fresh lettuce.

SERVES 6.

Do not alter the recipe or change the ingredients, or your results will not be the same.

❦ *Caviar-Stuffed Avocados*

1 package (3 ounces) cream cheese, softened
¼ cup mayonnaise (we recommend Kraft Real Mayonnaise)
½ cup celery, minced
2 teaspoons lemon juice
4 tablespoons caviar (we suggest red salmon caviar)
Dash hot sauce (we recommend Tabasco)
2 ripe avocados
1 bunch curly red-tipped lettuce

Into the softened cream cheese, blend the mayonnaise, celery, lemon juice, 3 tablespoons of the caviar, and the hot sauce. Mix well.

Cut the avocados lengthwise, remove the pit, and peel. Brush all over with lemon juice to prevent darkening. Line four salad plates with lettuce leaves and place half an avocado on each plate. Fill the hollow of the avocado with the cheese and caviar mixture, and garnish with the reserved caviar.

SERVES 4.

This makes an excellent salad or side dish for a hot summer day.

❦ Seafood Salad

1 large loaf sandwich bread (minus approximately 6 slices)
Softened butter or margarine
1 cup celery, diced
1 large onion, minced
1 pound white crabmeat (may substitute two 6½-ounce cans crabmeat, drained)
4 hard-boiled eggs, finely chopped
3 cups mayonnaise
2 cans (6½ ounces each) shrimp, drained (may substitute 1 pound small fresh shrimp, cooked and deveined)

Trim crust from bread, spread with butter, and cut into cubes. Add celery, onion, and egg, mix lightly and refrigerate overnight.

The next day, add mayonnaise, crab, and shrimp; mix gently and let stand 4 hours.

Serve with small party crackers of your choice. Will serve a party of about 30 people. For a smaller party, the recipe can easily be cut in half.

❦ Shrimp Salad

1 pound shrimp, boiled, peeled, and deveined
3 hard-boiled eggs, chopped
2 hearts of celery with tops, minced
2 tablespoons bell pepper, chopped
¼ teaspoon garlic salt
Salt, to taste
¼ teaspoon Tabasco sauce
½ cup mayonnaise
Juice of ½ lemon
1 tablespoon capers
¼ cup crackers or toasted bread crumbs

If the shrimp are large, cut into bite-sized pieces. Put the shrimp into a bowl. Add eggs, celery, bell pepper, garlic salt, salt, and Tabasco, and mix.

Add mayonnaise and lemon juice, and toss lightly. Sprinkle capers over top of salad.

If salad draws excess juice after tossing, gently add crackers or toasted bread crumbs just before serving.

SERVES 4.

Excellent served as a luncheon dish on a lettuce-lined plate.

❦ *Shrimp Mold*

1 can (10 ounces) tomato soup (not cream of tomato)
3 packages (3 ounces each) cream cheese
1 envelope gelatin (we suggest Knox)
¼ cup water
2 cups shrimp, boiled and cut up (may substitute frozen shrimp)
1 cup mayonnaise
1 small onion, grated
½ cup celery, finely chopped
Dash of garlic powder
Dash of salt and pepper
1 tablespoon lemon juice
1 teaspoon chives

Heat soup and dissolve cheese in hot soup. Soak gelatin in cold water. Add gelatin to soup and cool for 30 minutes.

Add remaining ingredients and mix well. Pour into an oiled 2-quart mold and chill, preferably overnight.

For a luncheon entrée, slice the shrimp mold and serve on plates lined with lettuce.

SERVES 6 TO 8.

To use as an appetizer, turn out onto a large platter and serve with crackers.

SERVES 20 OR MORE WITH OTHER APPETIZERS.

❦ Linda's Grilled Chicken and Spinach Salad

6 boneless, skinless chicken breasts
Garlic salt and pepper, to taste
1 lime, juiced
2 bunches fresh spinach, broken into bite-sized pieces
½ pound fresh mushrooms, sliced
1 purple onion, sliced thin into rings
1 pound cherry tomatoes, halved
½ pound cheddar cheese, grated
½ pound Swiss cheese, grated

DRESSING
⅓ cup olive oil
¼ cup red wine vinegar
½ teaspoon salt
¼ teaspoon freshly ground pepper
2 tablespoons Grey Poupon mustard

Season the chicken with garlic salt, pepper, and lime juice, and grill over a medium open fire or in a moderate oven until done. Cool the chicken and cut into strips. Mix the salad makings in a large bowl and top with the chicken pieces. Mix the Dressing and shake or stir well. Pour over the salad and toss.

SERVES 6.

❦ Antipasto, Ruby

MARINADE
¾ cup cold water
¾ cup red wine vinegar
¼ cup vegetable oil
2½ tablespoons sugar
2 cloves garlic, minced
1 teaspoon oregano
Salt and freshly ground pepper, to taste

½ head cauliflower, broken into small florets
2 carrots, julienned
3 stalks celery, cut in ½-inch pieces
1 bell pepper, cut in 1-inch strips
1 red bell pepper, cut in 1-inch strips
1 can (4 ounces) seedless black olives
6 very small onions
1 cup fresh, small, tender string beans, cut in half

In a large skillet or saucepan, combine the marinade ingredients and bring to a boil. Add all the vegetables and return the pan to a boil. Reduce heat and simmer for approximately 8 minutes. Remove from the heat and allow to cool. Place the antipasto in a covered container and refrigerate for 2 days.

SERVES 6.

This salad is excellent for cocktail parties or served as a first course on a lettuce-lined salad plate.

Entrées

MEATS

❦ *Chef Oscar's Salisbury Steak with Onion Gravy*

1 pound ground meat
¼ cup green onions, finely chopped
½ cup yellow onions, finely chopped
¼ cup fresh parsley, finely chopped
4 cloves garlic, minced
1 teaspoon black pepper
1 teaspoon garlic powder
1 teaspoon garlic salt
1 teaspoon onion powder
½ teaspoon Lawry's seasoned salt

Mix all of the ingredients together and shape into patties. Put the patties on a cookie sheet and bake in a 375-degree oven for 30 minutes (or cook in a skillet on top of the stove). Serve with Onion Gravy.

ONION GRAVY
1 large onion, diced
3 tablespoons flour
3 cups water
Salt and pepper, to taste

Sauté onion until tender. Add flour and stir until brown. Add water, stirring well. Salt and pepper to taste.
   Serve over steak.

SERVES 4.

This dish is excellent served with mashed potatoes.

❦ Cajun Rabbit Sauce Piquanté

1 teaspoon garlic powder, divided
1 teaspoon onion powder, divided
2 teaspoons freshly ground black pepper, divided
1 teaspoon white pepper, divided
2 teaspoons cayenne pepper, divided
2 teaspoons Lawry's seasoned salt, divided
3 whole fresh rabbits, cut in 6 pieces each
2 cups flour
2 cups peanut oil (we prefer Louana)
1 pound butter or margarine
3 cups onions, chopped fine
3 cups green onions, chopped fine
1½ whole heads garlic, minced
4 whole fresh tomatoes, peeled and diced
1 can (10 ounces) Rotel tomatoes, seasoned with jalapeño peppers
1 tablespoon salt
1 gallon Basic Chicken Stock (see page 187)

In a mixing bowl, combine ½ teaspoon garlic powder, ½ teaspoon onion powder, 1 teaspoon black pepper, ½ teaspoon white pepper, 1 teaspoon cayenne, and 1 teaspoon Lawry's seasoned salt. Mix well and set aside. Wash and drain the rabbit pieces, place them in a baking dish, and rub well with the mixed spices. Cover and refrigerate overnight.

When ready to prepare, dredge the rabbit pieces in flour, and brown in a small amount of peanut oil in a heavy skillet (we prefer cast iron). Drain the pieces well. Make a golden-brown Roux (see page 181) in the same skillet, using 1 cup flour and 1 cup peanut oil. This roux should be about the color of peanut butter or a little darker. Set the roux aside. In a large, heavy Dutch oven, melt the butter and cook the vegetables until they are tender. Add all the remaining spices, fresh tomatoes, and Rotel tomatoes and cook 30 minutes before adding 1 gallon of Basic Chicken Stock and the browned pieces of rabbit. Cook slowly until tender for about 1 hour. Do not let the meat get so tender that it falls off the bones. Now, add the roux and bring to a boil. Cook until the sauce thickens.

Serve with a mound of white rice and a green salad.

SERVES 9.

❦ Creole Meat Loaf

1½ pounds lean ground meat
1 cup tomato juice or catsup
¾ cup bread crumbs
2 eggs, beaten
¼ cup onion, chopped
1 teaspoon salt
¼ teaspoon pepper

Heat the oven to 350 degrees. Combine all of the ingredients in a large bowl and mix well. Press the mixture into a loaf pan and bake for 1 hour.
   To serve, top with Creole Sauce (see page 182) before serving.

SERVES 6 TO 8.

Miss Ruby's Creole Country Dinner, which is a real favorite with the locals, includes this meat loaf served with macaroni and cheese, a green vegetable (turnip greens, okra and tomatoes, or green beans), and cornbread.

❦ Baked Pork Loin

5 to 6 pounds pork loin roast (ask the butcher to crack the bone)
1 cup water
Salt and pepper, to taste

Salt and pepper the roast on all sides, rubbing the seasoning in well. Place the roast in a large baking dish and add the water. Bake uncovered for 1½ hours, or until the roast is fork-tender. Use the juice from the roast to baste the meat from time to time.
   Serve with sweet potatoes, Candied Yams (see page 163), or mashed potatoes and gravy, and a green vegetable. The leftovers are great!

SERVES 8.

❦ Chef Oscar's Veal in White Wine

2 pieces baby veal (5 to 6 ounces each, cut in strips ½ inch wide)
1 cup flour
¼ teaspoon white pepper
½ teaspoon salt
¼ teaspoon Lawry's seasoned salt
2 tablespoons margarine
6 large fresh mushrooms, sliced
¼ cup white wine
½ pound egg noodles (enriched Italian noodles are best)

Mix the flour with the seasonings and then dredge the veal in the seasoned flour. Sauté the veal in 1 tablespoon margarine in a saucepan until it is slightly brown and tender.

In the meantime, sauté the mushrooms in 1 tablespoon margarine and the white wine.

In a separate saucepan, heat 1½ cups Bechemel or White Wine Sauce (see page 183).

Cook the noodles according to the instructions on the package. Be sure not to overcook them. Place the noodles on a preheated serving platter. Top with the veal, white wine sauce, and sautéed mushrooms.

Serve with a fresh green vegetable and green salad.

SERVES 2.

❦ Cajun-Style Meatballs

1½ pounds ground meat
⅔ cup green pepper, chopped
1 cup white onion, chopped
¼ cup fresh parsley, chopped
4 cloves garlic, chopped fine
1 teaspoon white pepper
1 teaspoon black pepper
1 teaspoon garlic powder
1 teaspoon garlic salt
1 teaspoon onion powder
½ teaspoon cayenne pepper
1 teaspoon Lawry's seasoned salt
1 teaspoon creole seasoning (we use Tony's)
3 eggs
1 cup bread crumbs
½ cup Parmesan cheese, freshly grated

Mix all the ingredients together well. Roll into 2-ounce balls and bake in a 400-degree oven for 15 minutes.

Put the meatballs in Tomato Gravy (see page 177) and cook slowly for 15 more minutes. Serve in a chafing dish with plenty of napkins and toothpicks on the side.

MAKES APPROXIMATELY 50 MEATBALLS. SERVES 6 AS AN ENTRÉE.

I serve these meatballs at cocktail parties when hot hor d'oeuvres are requested.

❦ *Osabucco*

4 veal shanks or veal roast, cut 2 inches thick
Salt and pepper, to taste
1 cup flour
½ cup cooking oil
1 large onion, cut in chunks
6 carrots, cut in 2-inch pieces
4 stalks celery, cut in 3-inch pieces
1 pint white wine
1 tablespoon chicken base or chicken bouillon granules
1 tablespoon beef base or beef bouillon granules

Season the meat with salt and pepper, roll it in the flour, and brown it in oil in a heavy skillet. Add the onions and cook until limp. Place the meat into a large baking dish and add the celery, carrots, wine, chicken base, and beef base. Cover the meat with water. Then, cover the dish and cook in a slow oven for 2 hours. Uncover and brown. The gravy will be just thick enough to serve with egg noodles on the side.

SERVES 4.

This is a very old New Orleans family recipe. You'll love it!

❦ *Veal Oscar*

1 cup all purpose flour
Salt and freshly ground black pepper, to taste
4 baby white veal filets (6 ounces each)
¼ pound butter or margarine
1 can (10 ounces) whole green asparagus, heated (we suggest Green Giant)
     or
12 stalks fresh asparagus, lightly steamed
½ pound Lump Crabmeat Topping (see page 131)
1 cup Hollandaise Sauce (see page 187)

Mix the flour, salt, and pepper. Pound the veal with a mallet until thin and lightly coat with the seasoned flour. Heat the butter in a large iron skillet (use two skillets if necessary to keep from crowding the filets) and cook for 2 to 3 minutes on each side until lightly browned. Remove to a heated platter and place 3 stalks of hot asparagus on each filet. Top with Crabmeat Topping and Hollandaise Sauce.

Serve with Oven-Browned Potatoes (see page 152). This is always a very popular dish at *Miss Ruby's* and very pretty to serve.

SERVES 4.

❦ *Smoked Rack of Lamb*

2 racks of lamb (1½ pounds each)
Salt and freshly ground black pepper, to taste
1 log of pecan wood (12-inch length)

Have your butcher trim the racks of lamb for you. Start your grill with hickory or any other hardwood charcoal briquettes. When the fire is very hot, start the pecan log and let it begin to burn and smoke. Salt and pepper the racks and place them on the grill for 10 to 12 minutes. Turn them frequently to keep them from burning. When they come from the grill, they will be rare. Take the racks to the kitchen and cut apart. If further cooking is needed, run the chops under the broiler (medium-rare, 6 minutes; medium, 8 minutes; well-done, 12 minutes) and turn them several times. Serve 3 chops per person.

SERVES 4 TO 5.

These chops are truly the best in the world! The unforgettable taste come from the pecan wood. One of my favorite restaurants here in New Orleans serves this dish and they always know what I've come for when they see me walk in the door. Serve with mint jelly, fresh broccoli, baby carrots and, of course, a green salad.

❦ Chef Oscar's Beef Stroganoff

4 pound sirloin tip roast (or any lean beef roast)
2 teaspoons black pepper
1 teaspoon white pepper
1 teaspoon Lawry's seasoned salt
1 teaspoon garlic salt
2 teaspoons garlic powder
1 teaspoon salt
2 cups onion, finely chopped
1 cup celery, finely chopped
5 cloves garlic, finely chopped
1 cup bell pepper, chopped
1 cup flour
1½ gallons beef stock
1½ tablespoons Kitchen Bouquet
1½ tablespoons chicken base or chicken bouillon granules
1½ cups fresh mushrooms, sliced
1 cup sour cream

Dice the meat into small pieces (1- to 1½-ounce cubes), mix with the first six spices, and place in a large pan. Brown in the oven at 475 degrees for 35 minutes. Add the chopped vegetables (the next four ingredients) and cook for 20 minutes or more. Stir in the flour and cook another 15 minutes.

Stir in the beef stock, Kitchen Bouquet, chicken base, and mushrooms. Cook 1½ hours or until the meat is tender. Lastly, add the sour cream and serve over egg noodles.

SERVES 8.

❦ Boiled Dinner

2 cans (10½ ounces) beef broth
2 cans (10½ ounces) chicken broth
2 cans water
2 pounds lean beef brisket
1 roasting chicken (about 4 pounds), cut into pieces
1 onion, diced
Bouquet Garni (see page 184)
4 potatoes, peeled and quartered
2 carrots, scraped and halved lengthwise
¾ pound green beans, trimmed and tied in a bunch
2 zucchini, sliced
4 cooked beets
1 teaspoon fresh parsley, chopped

Bring the beef and chicken broths with the water to a boil in a Dutch oven or a large pot. Add the brisket and the chicken and bring to a boil again; be sure that the liquid completely covers the brisket and the chicken. Add the onion and the Bouquet Garni, reduce heat, and simmer for 1½ hours.

Add the potatoes and carrots, making sure the broth covers all the ingredients Simmer for 25 minutes more and then add the green beans. Simmer for approximately 8 minutes; then, add the zucchini and continue simmering for another 8 to 10 minutes.

Meanwhile, quarter the beets and heat them in a small saucepan. Place the meat and chicken on a preheated platter, and surround with the vegetables. Drain the beets thoroughly and arrange them next to the beef. Sprinkle with the fresh parsley.

SERVES 6 TO 8.

❦ Chef Oscar's Stuffed Leg of Lamb

1 leg of lamb with bone in (10 pounds)
2 tablespoons butter or margarine
1½ pounds lean ground beef
1 pound creole smoked sausage or any good Polish sausage
2½ cups white onions, chopped very fine
2 cups green onions, sliced very thin
1 cup fresh parsley, chopped fine
1 cup bell pepper, chopped very fine
1 whole head garlic, minced
2 teaspoons garlic salt
1½ teaspoons Lawry's seasoned salt
1½ teaspoon white pepper
2 teaspoons garlic powder
2 teaspoons onion powder
½ teaspoon cayenne pepper
½ teaspoon oregano
1½ cups unseasoned bread crumbs
1 bunch celery, cut in 2 inch pieces
2 large onions, quartered
2 cups water
Brown Butter Sauce (see page 185)

Trim most of the fat off of the lamb and debone. If you have the butcher debone the leg, be sure to ask him for the bones. Spread the deboned meat on a chopping block and beat vigorously with a mallet until it is flat because you are going to make a roll with it. Wash well and pat dry. Trim off most of the visible fat, muscles, and stringy parts. Set the meat aside.

For the dressing, melt the butter or margarine in a heavy skillet or sauté pan and brown the ground meat over medium heat. While the meat is cooking, remove the skin from the sausage and chop in a food processor. Add to the ground meat and stir in well. Add the onion, parsley, bell pepper, garlic, garlic salt, Lawry's seasoned salt, white pepper, garlic powder, onion powder, cayenne pepper, and oregano, and cook until the vegetables are tender. Stir frequently while cooking. Remove from the heat and add the bread crumbs.

Spread the lamb out on a tray (preferably stainless) and pat it down until flat. Place the dressing in the center of the meat and make a roll by turning one side at a time over the dressing. Tuck in the ends to make a neat package. Cover tightly with foil and refrigerate overnight or at least 10 to 12 hours.

The next day, remove the lamb from the refrigerator and tie around it with kitchen string at 1- to 1½-inch intervals and then from end to end about three times. Place the lamb in a large baking pan and surround it with the bones, celery, quartered onions and water. Cover tightly with foil and bake in a 400-degree oven for 1 hour.

After 1 hour, take the lamb out of the oven and remove the foil. Baste and return to the oven to cook for 1 hour more. Baste every 15 minutes during this last hour of cooking to insure a beautiful, even, golden-brown crust. (Use a basting bulb to prevent burning yourself.) When done, remove the meat from the oven and let it sit for about 15 minutes before slicing.

Place 2 tablespoons of Brown Butter Sauce in the center of each pre-heated plate and lay one slice in the sauce. Garnish with a sprig of fresh parsley and serve with Oven-Browned Potatoes (see page 152), a green vegetable and a crispy green salad.

SERVES 8 TO 10.

Watching Chef Oscar prepare this dish in my kitchen is like watching an artist create a masterpiece. He follows no recipe. He just creates! Chef Oscar has cooked in many of New Orleans's finest restaurants and worked with us for 5½ years. He says working with us was the high-light of his career because we believe in buying and serving only the very finest and freshest food on the market.

❦ *Daube Glace*

2½ pounds boneless beef chuck
1½ pounds boneless pork loin
Salt and freshly ground black pepper, to taste
3 tablespoons bacon grease or margarine
2 veal knuckle bones, cut in three pieces each
3 onions, sliced
3 carrots, sliced
12 cloves garlic, minced
½ bunch fresh parsley, chopped
6 medium bay leaves
1 teaspoon thyme
1¼ cups celery, coarsely chopped
¾ teaspoon allspice
½ teaspoon cayenne pepper
3½ cups Beef Stock (see page 186)
2 cups water
⅓ cup brandy
1 cup dry white wine
5 envelopes Knox gelatin
1½ cups water
5 tablespoons fresh lemon juice
1 tablespoon salt
½ teaspoon Tabasco sauce
3 tablespoons Worcestershire sauce (we prefer Lea & Perrin's)
1 tablespoon Lawry's seasoned salt
2 teaspoons white pepper
½ cup pimientos, finely chopped

Remove the fat from the meat and season with salt and pepper. Put the bacon grease or margarine in a large Dutch oven over high heat and brown the meat on all sides. When the meat is browned, remove and pour off any remaining fat. Put the bones into the pot and brown them slightly. Then, add the meat, onion, carrots, garlic, parsley, bay leaves, thyme, celery, allspice, and cayenne pepper, and mix well. Then, add the Beef Stock, water, brandy, and wine. Bring to a boil, cover, and simmer for 3 to 3½ hours. Remove the meat and set aside. Strain the stock through a colander and then through two layers of cheesecloth, and set aside in a large, clean pot. Let the stock set until the fat comes to the top and then skim it off. Meanwhile, dice the meats.

Place the gelatin in 1½ cups water to dissolve and add to the hot stock. Then, add the lemon juice, salt, Tabasco sauce, Worcestershire sauce, white pepper, and pimiento, and stir well. The stock should have a spicy, salty taste because the meat will absorb the seasoning as it jells.

Lightly oil two Pyrex loaf pans and divide the meats between them. Add the stock slowly, cover, and refrigerate overnight or until firmly jelled. Before serving, skim any grease off the top and turn out onto a platter. Garnish with finely chopped fresh parsley and very thin slices of lemon. Slice with a sharp knife in ½-inch pieces to serve as an appetizer, or cut larger slices for a main course. This dish is delightful for a hot summer lunch or supper. Try Garlic Mayonnaise (see page 178) with it.

This is a very old French recipe.

❦ *Beef Pot Roast*

4 to 5 pounds beef chuck roast, boneless
2 yellow onions, sliced
4 stalks celery, sliced
6 potatoes, quartered
6 carrots, cut into rounds
Salt and pepper, to taste

Salt and pepper the roast on each side. Place the roast into a large baking pan or Dutch oven. Arrange the onion and celery in strips on top and around the roast. Add 1 cup of water to the pan and cover. Bake at 400 degrees for 1½ hours, or until the roast is almost tender. Add the potatoes and carrots around the roast, cover, and cook for 45 minutes or more until the potatoes and carrots are tender.

SERVES 8 TO 10.

This roast is one of the best, and it's wonderful warmed over.

❦ Deluxe Hamburger
from Miss Ruby's Other Place

2 pounds lean ground beef (we prefer top round, ground once)
Salt and freshly ground black pepper, to taste
1 teaspoon Lawry's seasoned salt
12 slices bacon
1 pound fresh mushrooms, sliced
2 tablespoons butter or margarine
1 large sweet onion, thinly sliced
2 large fresh tomatoes, sliced
1 head iceberg lettuce
6 slices American cheese
4 Kosher dill pickles, thinly sliced
6 large hamburger buns

Put the ground meat in a mixing bowl, sprinkle with salt, pepper, and Lawry's seasoned salt, and mix thoroughly by hand. Set aside. Assemble your choice of condiments and set aside. Fry the bacon until crisp and drain on a paper towel. Sauté the mushrooms in 2 tablespoons butter and set aside. Slice the onion and tomatoes, and arrange with the lettuce leaves on a large platter along with the cheese and dill pickles.

Form 6 patties and grill over charcoal or in a heavy skillet that has been lightly greased until the desired doneness is reached. Place the meat on a toasted bun that has been spread with mayonnaise (we prefer Kraft's Real Mayonnaise), mustard, and catsup as desired. Add the cheese, bacon, mushrooms, tomato, onion, and lettuce.

SERVES 6.

This is a balanced meal and truly the best hamburger you will ever eat. Serve with French fries and a pickle spear on the side. It will certainly please any man in your life.

❦ Braised Creole Beef Rump Roast

1 boneless beef rump roast (3 to 4 pounds)
2 tablespoons bacon drippings
2 tablespoons chili sauce (we prefer Hunt's)
2 tablespoons water
1 cube beef bouillon
2 cloves garlic, minced
1 teaspoon salt
¼ teaspoon dry mustard
1 bay leaf
6 drops Tabasco sauce
1 can (16 ounces) whole tomatoes, cut into pieces
1 can (14 ounces) artichoke hearts, drained
1 cup green onions, sliced
¼ cup Parmesan cheese
2 tablespoons fresh parsley, chopped
1 teaspoon lemon juice
3 tablespoons flour

Brown the roast in the bacon drippings in a heavy Dutch oven. Pour off the drippings and add the chili sauce, water, bouillon, garlic, salt, dry mustard, bay leaf, and Tabasco sauce. Cover and cook in a 325-degree oven for 1 hour and 45 minutes, or until tender. Then add the tomatoes (reserving the liquid), artichoke hearts, green onion, Parmesan cheese, parsley, and lemon juice to the pot. Cover and bake for 15 minutes more. Remove the meat and the artichoke hearts to a hot serving platter. Blend the tomato liquid with flour and use to thicken the sauce.

SERVES 6 TO 8.

This recipe is also good with round steak or pot roast.

❦ *Lasagna*

1 package (16 ounces) lasagna noodles
1 tablespoon olive oil
1 teaspoon salt

MEAT SAUCE
½ pound Italian sausage
2 tablespoons olive oil
2 pounds ground meat
2 cups Italian Tomato Sauce (see page 177)
2 bay leaves
1 teaspoon fresh garlic, minced
1 tablespoon chicken base or chicken bouillon granules
2 generous dashes Worcestershire sauce
Dash cayenne pepper
¼ cup fresh parsley, finely chopped
⅓ cup Parmesan or Romano cheese, freshly ground

CHEESE FILLING AND FINAL INGREDIENTS
1 whole egg
1½ pints ricotta cheese
1 teaspoon fresh parsley, finely chopped
1 tablespoon Parmesan or Romano cheese, freshly ground
¾ teaspoon fresh garlic, minced
½ pound mozzarella cheese, thinly sliced
½ cup Italian Tomato Sauce (see page 177)
Italian Tomato Gravy (see page 177)

Boil the lasagna noodles in a large pot with the olive oil and salt for approximately 20 minutes. Drain the noodles and separate. Set aside.

Squeeze the Italian sausage out of its casing. In a large pot, sauté the sausage in olive oil for 5 minutes. Add the ground beef and continue to sauté for 15 minutes. Drain off fat.

Add the Italian Tomato Sauce, bay leaves, garlic, chicken base or bouillon, Worcestershire sauce, cayenne pepper, parsley and cheese. Simmer for 20 minutes over low heat.

In a mixing bowl, beat the egg. Add the ricotta cheese, parsley, Parmesan or Romano cheese, and garlic. Mix well.

In a Pyrex baking dish, assemble layers in the following order:
1. Layer of overlapping noodles
2. Meat sauce
3. Ricotta cheese mixture, in dollops
4. Layer of overlapping sliced mozzarella cheese
5. Light sprinkle of Parmesan or Romano cheese
6. Noodles
7. Meat sauce
8. Cheese mixture
9. Noodles
10. Italian Tomato Sauce smoothed over noodles
11. Overlapping mozzarella cheese
12. Sprinkle of Parmesan or Romano cheese

Bake at 350 degrees for 30 to 45 minutes. After cooking, allow to cool for 45 minutes before cutting into 3-inch squares (this should prevent the lasagna from sliding apart). Just before serving, place each square in an ovenproof ramekin and pour some Italian Tomato Gravy over each serving. Top with some grated cheese and heat until bubbly hot.

SERVES 6 TO 8.

This freezes well. Cut into serving pieces and wrap separately. You may also freeze the tomato sauce in a separate container.

❦ Miss Ruby's Traditional Couscous

1¼-pound boneless lamb or 1 large stewing hen
1 large can (46 ounces) tomato juice
Salt and pepper, to taste
⅝ ounces cumin
1 dried red pepper
1½ cups diced rutabaga, turnips, and potatoes
⅞ cup carrots, diced
1¾ cups zucchini, diced
1¼ cups Pattypan squash (a flat, white squash)
1½ small onions, diced
1 can (16 ounces) tomatoes
1 tablespoon butter
½ teaspoon ginger
2 teaspoons cloves
⅛ teaspoon nutmeg
⅛ teaspoon cinnamon
2 cloves garlic, minced
¼ cup golden raisins
1 cup garbanzo beans, cooked and drained
2 pounds couscous

THE STOCK
Put the lamb or the hen into a large pot filled with 2 quarts of water. Simmer the meat for several hours. Skim off the fat. If you choose chicken, remove when the meat is quite tender and bone. Discard the bones and skin, and cut the meat into roughly 1½-inch cubes. Add half the tomato juice to the stock (add more while cooking if needed to keep the proportion of liquid to vegetables high). Simmer the broth; add 1½ tablespoons salt (or to taste), ¾ teaspoon cumin, and half the red pepper.

THE VEGETABLES
Peel the vegetables (except the squash and zucchini), cut into cubes, and set aside.

THE MEAT
Melt the butter and stir in the ginger, cloves, nutmeg, cinnamon, and garlic. Stir this mixture into the meat, but *do not brown*. Simply warm and glaze the meat in the spices. Remove the meat from the heat and set it aside.

THE PREPARATION

An hour and 15 minutes before serving, add the rutabaga, carrots, and potatoes to the stock. One hour before, add the turnips and onions. Forty-five minutes before, add the meat, golden raisins, and garbanzo beans. Thirty minutes before, add the zucchini, squash, and tomatoes. Add more tomato juice to maintain a high proportion of liquid. This mixture should be soupy. Add salt, cumin, and red pepper to taste.

THE COUSCOUS GRAIN

Thirty minutes before serving, combine 1 cup of warm water and ½ teaspoon salt for each pound of grain. Pour the grain in a large bowl and cover with water. Let stand for 3 minutes until the water is absorbed, then crumble the grain between your fingers, breaking up any lumps. Put the grain in a metal colander lined with cheesecloth and place over a large pot of rapidly boiling water. Cover the colander with a large lid so the steam rises through it and the grain. Wrap the sides in foil if necessary to seal and to keep the steam from escaping anywhere but through the top. Steam for 5 to 10 minutes.

TO SERVE

Serve the stew over grain with harissa sauce (a thick hot sauce). I prefer to use salsa or Basque Salsa (see page 181) instead.

SERVES 8.

❦ Blackened Steak

4 prime rib eye steaks, 1 inch thick (16 ounces)
4 teaspoons Blackened Seasoning (see page 3)
¼ pound butter or margarine (if skillet method is used)

Rub the seasoning into the meat (if you like it spicy, add more). Heat an outdoor grill or melt the butter in a heavy iron skillet. When the skillet is very hot, add the steaks and cook to the desired doneness. If you cook indoors, be sure to run your vent on high as the Blackened Seasoning tends to smoke a great deal.

❦ Miss Jean's Famous Prime Rib Roast au Jus

1 teaspoon Lawry's seasoned salt
½ teaspoon salt
1 teaspoon black pepper
1 teaspoon Tony's seasoning
½ teaspoon garlic salt
6-pound boneless rib eye
1 cup water
1 teaspoon Worcestershire sauce (we recommend Lea & Perrin's)

Mix the dry seasonings together in a bowl. Sprinkle the seasoning mixture on all sides of the roast, and rub well into the meat. Place the roast in a baking dish and pour the water and the Worcestershire sauce around it. Bake uncovered in a 450-degree oven for 1 hour. *Turn the oven off*, and leave the roast in the oven undisturbed until 30 minutes before serving.

Then, heat the roast for 30 minutes in a 350-degree oven. The roast will be medium-rare. If you desire either rare or well-done meat, adjust the cooking time accordingly. Serve in hot au-jus.

SERVES 8.

❦ Bar-B-Que Brisket

3 to 4 pounds beef brisket, trimmed
1 teaspoon salt
2 teaspoons celery seed
1 teaspoon garlic powder
2 teaspoons Worcestershire sauce (we recommmend Lea & Perrin's)
1 teaspoon onion salt
2 teaspoons black pepper
1 teaspoon white pepper
2 tablespoons liquid smoke
2 tablespoons cider vinegar
1 cup or more Bar-B-Que Sauce (see page 180)

Mix the salt, celery seed, garlic powder, Worcestershire sauce, onion salt, pepper, liquid smoke, and vinegar together in a bowl. Spread the mixture on both sides of the brisket. Place the brisket, fat side up, in a Pyrex dish. Cover with foil and refrigerate overnight.

The next day, spread on the Bar-B-Que Sauce, wrap tightly in heavy-duty foil, and bake in a 275-degree oven for 4 to 5 hours. The foil should be removed for the last hour of cooking.

To serve, slice the brisket very thinly and top with a little extra sauce.

SERVES 8 TO 10.

Bar-B-Que Brisket is great with potato salad, and it makes a wonderful party dish!

🍒 Italian Meatballs and Spaghetti Sauce

MEATBALLS
2 pounds ground lean meat (ground twice)
1½ onions, finely chopped
2 cups bread crumbs (French bread is best}
6 eggs
2 bunches fresh parsley, chopped
1 tablespoon crushed red pepper
Salt and black pepper, to taste
1 tablespoon Ac'cent flavor enhancer (optional)
1 bunch green onions, finely chopped

Mix all the ingredients together well. Roll the mixture into 2-ounce balls and bake in a 400-degree oven for 30 minutes.

SPAGHETTI SAUCE
3 cans (16 ounces each) whole tomatoes
1 can (6 ounces) tomato paste
2 tablespoons chopped fresh basil or 1 tablespoon dried basil
1 teaspoon thyme
3 cloves garlic, chopped (optional)

Put all of the ingredients into a blender or a food processor and blend well. Place in a heavy saucepan and cook slowly for 1 hour or more.

When the meatballs are cooked, they may be heated in the sauce before serving over spaghetti.

SERVES 8.

❦ Linda's Famous Oklahoma Chili

5 pounds lean beef, coarsely ground
Salt and freshly ground black pepper, to taste
4 large onions, chopped
2 green bell peppers, chopped
6 stalks celery, chopped
8 cloves garlic, minced
8 cans (10 ounces each) Rotel tomatoes, seasoned with jalapeño peppers
6 cans (15 ounces each) stewed tomatoes
½ cup water
½ teaspoon William's chili seasoning (or any good brand)
2 teaspoons ground cumin
Crushed red pepper, to taste
1 can (15 ounces) chili beans
1 can (12 ounces) sliced mushrooms
½ cup grated cheddar cheese
½ cup green onions, finely chopped (optional)

Season the ground meat with salt and pepper. Brown the seasoned meat in a large skillet with the onion, green pepper, celery, and garlic until it's done and the celery is tender. Drain off the fat and transfer the mixture to a large chili pot. Add the cans of tomatoes until you have enough juice. Use the water if needed and then add the chili seasoning, ground cumin, and red pepper to taste. Simmer for two hours, stirring occasionally. Then add the chili beans and sliced mushrooms, and cook for 30 minutes more.
  Serve topped with grated cheddar cheese and chopped green onion.

This chili recipe was given to me by my good friends from Norman, Oklahoma, Linda Lake Young and her husband, Robert. It is the very best chili and freezes well. We always make a big pot of Linda's chili when they visit me here in New Orleans. Some of my fondest memories come from our visits while we are cooking and enjoying our refreshments.

❦ Pepper Steak

1 round steak, cut in strips or cubed
2 tablespoons butter or margarine
2 bell peppers, chopped
1 large onion, coarsely chopped
⅛ teaspoon garlic powder
1 beef bouillon cube
1 can (10 ounces) Rotel tomatoes, seasoned with jalapeño peppers
2 tablespoons soy sauce
½ teaspoon sugar
1 tablespoon cornstarch
2 tablespoons water

Brown the steak in the butter or margarine. Add the bell peppers, onion, and garlic powder, and continue to cook. After browning, add the bouillon cube and tomatoes.

Mix the soy sauce, sugar, cornstarch, and water together. Add to the steak and simmer for about 30 minutes until the meat is tender, and the sauce is glossy and thick.

Serve over rice.

SERVES 6.

POULTRY

🐦 *Betsy's Quail in Cognac*

8 quail
Salt and freshly ground black pepper, to taste
1 cup flour
1 stick butter
8 green onions, whole
1 cup chicken stock
½ cup cognac
½ cup green onions, finely chopped
¼ cup chopped celery
¼ cup bell pepper, chopped
¼ cup mushroom stems, chopped
1 cup whole mushroom caps
1 bunch fresh parsley or watercress

Wash the quail and pat them dry. Salt, pepper, and lightly flour each bird. Melt the butter in a deep sauté pan or heavy skillet and brown the quail on all sides. Transfer the birds to a large baking dish and insert one whole green onion in the cavity of each. Pour ½ cup chicken stock and ¼ cup cognac over the birds, and cover with foil. Bake in a 325-degree oven for about 45 minutes or until tender. Meanwhile, add the chopped vegetables to the drippings in the sauté pan or skillet that you browned the quail in and cook until tender. Add the remaining chicken stock and cognac, and reduce the liquid to the desired consistency. When the quail are done, strain the sauce (gravy) over the birds, mashing the vegetables against the side of the strainer to release all of the juices; discard the mashed vegetables. Sauté the mushroom caps in a small amount of butter and use them as garnish with parsley or watercress on the platter. Excess sauce (gravy) should be served in a sauceboat.

SERVES 4 TO 8.

Delicious served with wild rice.

❦ Turkey Poulette

1 pound sliced turkey breast
3 stalks celery
1 large onion

CHEESE SAUCE
3 tablespoons butter
2 tablespoons vegetable oil
6 heaping tablespoons flour
1 can (12 ounces) evaporated milk
4 cans (12 ounces each) water
6 ounces American cheese or Velveeta
8 ounces fresh mushrooms, sliced
⅛ teaspoon yellow food coloring
Pepper and Lawry's seasoned salt, to taste

8 slices bread, toasted
1 cup cheddar cheese, coarsely grated
8 slices thick-sliced bacon, crisply fried

Miss Ruby always bakes her own turkey breast for this New Orleans favorite. She uses a whole turkey breast and stuffs it with onion and celery. The breast is then placed inside of a plain brown paper bag, put in a pan, and baked at 350 degrees for 25 minutes per pound of turkey.

In a pot, melt 3 tablespoons butter and oil together. Add the flour and make a white roux (see Roux, page 181). Do not brown the roux; it should be a light creamy color. Add the evaporated milk and water to the roux and stir. Add the cheese and stir constantly while the cheese melts to prevent sticking. Add the mushrooms and food coloring, and continue stirring. The cheese sauce should be of a lightly thickened consistency.

Cut the toast into points and arrange on ovensafe plates or in a baking dish. Allow two pieces of toast per person. Arrange the turkey over the toast points. Pour a generous amount of cheese sauce over the turkey. The cheese sauce should cover the turkey and the toast entirely. Sprinkle the cheddar cheese over the top. Run the open-faced sandwiches under the broiler, and broil until the cheddar cheese begins to brown. Garnish with a strip of bacon on each side of the sandwiches and serve immediately.

Broccoli makes a very tasty side dish for Turkey Poulette, and it adds to the colorful appearance of the dish.

SERVES 4.

This is an old New Orleans favorite that has vanished from most menus. It is a wonderful brunch, lunch, or after-theater dish. The sauce can be made a day ahead if kept refrigerated.

❦ *Miss Ruby's Special Baked Turkey*

1 turkey, 10 to 12 pounds
1 teaspoon freshly ground black pepper
1½ teaspoons salt
2 teaspoons Lawry's seasoned salt
1 bunch celery, cut in 2-inch pieces
2 large onions, quartered

Remove the giblets, wash the turkey inside and out, and pat it dry. Rub the seasonings inside the turkey cavity and the neck, and sprinkle on the outside, patting or rubbing the seasonings into the skin.

Stuff the cavities with the onion and celery, and close the skin on the neck cavity. Slide the turkey into a large plain brown paper bag and staple the top closed. Place the bagged turkey in a large baking pan and cook for 3 to 4 hours in a 350-degree oven. To check for doneness, tear the bag from the top. When the legs begin to pull away from the body, the turkey is done or, if you have a pop-up timer, follow it. This method will assure a moist, browned bird every time. Baste the bird with its own juice and enjoy. Turkey breasts can also be cooked carefree this way.

Miss Ruby says that the turkey will smell so good while it is cooking that you will never forget it. Serve with Cornbread Dressing (see page 120) and Giblet Gravy (see page 179).

❦ Cornish Hens with Southern Dressing

¼ cup raisins
½ cup sauterne
4 Cornish game hens
1½ teaspoons Lawry's seasoned salt
1 cup butter or margarine
1¼ cups onions, chopped
2 cups crumbled cornbread
1 teaspoon salt
Freshly ground pepper, to taste
¼ teaspoon poultry seasoning
2 eggs, beaten
¾ cup chopped pecans
1 cup wild rice
3 cups water
1 pound fresh mushrooms, sliced

Soak the raisins in the sauterne overnight and thaw the Cornish hens. The next day, wash the hens and sprinkle inside and out with Lawry's seasoned salt. In a small saucepan, melt ¼ cup butter, add half the onion, and sauté until tender. Place the crumbled cornbread in a large mixing bowl and add the raisin mixture, ½ teaspoon salt, pepper, poultry seasoning, eggs, and pecans. Mix well. Brush the cavities of the Cornish hens with melted butter and stuff them with the dressing. Place them in a shallow baking dish and bake in a 350-degree oven for 1 hour or until the hens are tender. Brush the hens with melted butter every 15 minutes while they cook.

While the hens bake, sauté the remaining onion in ¼ cup of butter until they are tender. Wash the rice well and drain. Pour 3 cups of water into a heavy pot and add the remaining ½ teaspoon of salt. Bring the salted water to a boil and stir in the rice gradually. Then, stir in the onion and cover. Cook for 30 minutes stirring from time to time. Sauté the mushrooms in the remaining butter and add to the rice mixture. Add more boiling water to the rice if needed. Cover and cook for 15 minutes more, or until the rice is tender and the water is absorbed. Serve the rice with the hens and use some of the broth from the baking pan for additional flavor.

SERVES 4.

Variation: Season the hens inside and out with Lawry's seasoned salt and freshly ground black pepper. Cut two onions in quarters and fill the cavities with the onion and one short piece of celery. Bake as above and serve with a mound of white rice, seasoned with some of the broth from the baking pan.
Either way you choose to cook them, Cornish Hens are delicious.

❦ Baked Chicken in White Wine

1 fryer (3½ to 4 pounds)
½ cup white wine (any kind)
¼ cup water
Salt, pepper, and Lawry's seasoned salt, to taste
4 stalks celery
2 medium yellow onions

Cut the fryer into quarters. Sprinkle on salt, pepper, and seasoned salt to taste and place it in a baking dish. Cut the celery and onion in strips and lay on top and around the chicken. Pour the wine and water around the chicken and bake uncovered in a 350-degree oven for 1 hour and 15 minutes, or until tender.

SERVES 4.

This poultry dish is very good served with rice or Cornbread Dressing (see page 120) with gravy and a green vegetable.

❦ Coq-au-Vin

2 fryers (3 pounds each), cut into serving pieces
¼ cup flour
Salt and freshly ground black pepper, to taste
Pinch of nutmeg
Pinch of paprika
1 stick butter or margarine
6 green onions, sliced
1 clove garlic, crushed
1 bay leaf
Pinch of thyme
½ cup sliced mushrooms
2 slices bacon, fried crisp
1½ cups burgundy wine

Mix the flour and all of the dry seasonings together in a bowl. Melt the butter in a large skillet. Dredge the chicken pieces in the flour mixture and fry lightly in the butter. When all the pieces are slightly cooked, place them in a casserole. Sauté the green onions and garlic in the skillet and put them over the chicken. Add the bay leaf, thyme, and mushrooms, and simmer for 15 minutes. Add the diced bacon and the wine. Bake in a 325-degree oven for 2 hours.

Serve with rice on the side.

SERVES 6 TO 8.

Several years ago, I met a professional chef who was vacationing here in New Orleans. He wanted to prepare this dish for me, so we went to the French Market and bought the ingredients. People passing by on the street wanted to know what we were cooking because it smelled so good.

❦ Chicken Cordon Bleu

1 cup margarine
6 ounces cooked ham, cubed
1 cup green onions, chopped
1 teaspoon black pepper
½ teaspoon chicken base or chicken-flavored bouillon by Knorr
¼ cup flour
½ cup milk
4 whole boneless chicken breasts, with skin
4 slices American cheese

EGG WASH
2 whole eggs
1 cup milk
¼ teaspoon salt

Melt margarine in a skillet. Add chopped ham and sauté for 5 minutes. Add onion, black pepper, and chicken base, and cook for 10 minutes. Add the flour and milk, stirring until well-mixed. Cook 10 minutes more and remove from heat.

Spread chicken breast on a cutting board, skin side down. Be sure to leave the skin on. Flatten each chicken breast with a mallet in order to make it easier to roll. On each breast, lay one slice of cheese. Put 2 tablespoons of the above dressing into each breast. Roll up like a jelly roll and close with toothpicks. Place the breasts on a cookie sheet and place either in the refrigerator or the freezer. Freezing helps to hold them together. If you freeze, them take them out of the freezer 30 minutes or so before cooking.

Combine all the egg wash ingredients and beat together well with a whisk. Dip the breasts in the egg wash, then roll them in a seasoned flour (flour with salt and pepper to taste, and a dash of cayenne). Dip the breasts into the egg wash again, and then roll in bread crumbs. Deep-fry in peanut oil, enough to cover the breasts, or bake in the oven 30 minutes at 375 degrees or until done. Serve with Brown Butter Sauce (see page 185).

SERVES 4.

❦ *Long Island Duck*

1 Long Island duck, 4 to 5 pounds
1 teaspoon Lawry's seasoned salt
Freshly ground pepper, to taste
2 onions, quartered
½ orange, cut in wedges
2 stalks celery hearts, with leaves
6 sprigs fresh parsley
3 carrots, sliced in 2-inch pieces
1 bay leaf
6 pepper corns
½ teaspoon salt
2 cups water
2 tablespoons butter or margarine
1¼ cups red wine
2 tablespoons flour

Remove the giblets and set aside; wash the duck well and pat it dry. Rub the duck inside and out with Lawry's seasoned salt and pepper. Stuff 1 onion, the orange wedges, 1 stalk of celery, and 3 sprigs of parsley into the duck's cavities and close the openings with metal skewers. Preheat the oven to 450 degrees and place the prepared duck in a baking pan, breast side up. Roast for 45 minutes and then turn the duck. Remove the fat from the pan and reserve the drippings. Roast for another 45 minutes, and again remove the fat and reserve the drippings. Reduce the oven temperature to 400 degrees and return the duck to the oven for another 45 minutes, breast side up. Baste every 15 minutes with the strained broth.

While the duck is cooking, place the giblets, 1 onion, 1 stalk of celery, the carrots, bay leaf, peppercorns, salt, water, and 1 cup of red wine in a saucepan and simmer for 45 minutes. Strain into another pan. This becomes the basting sauce for the duck.

Melt the butter in a heavy skillet and stir in the flour to make a light-brown roux. When the proper color is reached, add ¼ cup red wine and the drippings from the baking pan (without grease), and simmer until thickened. Serve in a gravy boat.

For a variation, mix together frozen orange juice concentrate and cranberry jelly. Spread over the duck during the last few minutes of baking. The duck will come out a beautiful golden-brown.

SERVES 4.

You will find this produces a beautiful, crisp, brown bird. Roast Duck is one of my favorites. This recipe came from a chef in Vancouver, B.C. We have served Long Island Duck for many private dinners and everyone loves it.

❦ *Mom's Southern Fried Chicken*

1 large whole fryer, plump
1 teaspoon Lawry's seasoned salt
1 teaspoon creole seasoning (we prefer Tony's)
1 teaspoon black pepper
2 cups all-purpose flour
2 eggs
1 cup milk
Peanut oil (amount depends on method used)

Mix the seasonings with the flour and set aside. Put the eggs in a bowl and beat with a wire whisk. Blend in the milk to make the "egg wash." Cut the chicken in eight pieces. Wash it well and pat dry. Heat the oil in a deep-fat fryer (325 degrees) or in a heavy skillet (cast iron preferred).

If you use the skillet method, only a small amount of oil will be needed — enough to come up to the sides of the pieces of chicken. Place the chicken in the egg wash, roll in the flour mixture until well-coated, and drop into the hot oil. Be sure that the grease is not too hot so that it will cook through without burning. Brown on both sides and then cover the skillet for about 15 minutes. Remove the lid and continue to cook until crispy and brown.

If you use a deep-fat fryer, cook the chicken until golden-brown; it will float to the top when it is done. Then, cook for about 2 minutes more.

NOTE: When seasoned flour is used for dredging and some is left, sift and freeze for future use.

❦ Ballotine of Duck

1 duck (4 or 5 pounds)
2 tablespoons oil
¼ pound small mushrooms, sliced
1 tablespoon butter
Trussing needle and string

STUFFING
2 tablespoons butter
1 onion, finely chopped
¾ pound pork or veal, ground
¾ cup fresh white bread crumbs
2 teaspoons parsley, finely chopped
1 teaspoon sage
¼ cup sherry
¼ pound cooked ham, shredded
2 tablespoons pistachio nuts, blanched and shredded
1 egg, beaten
Salt and pepper, to taste

ESPAGNOLE SAUCE
2 tablespoons oil
1 tablespoon carrots, finely diced
1 tablespoon onions, finely diced
½ tablespoon celery, finely diced
1½ tablespoons flour
2 cups chicken stock
½ teaspoon tomato paste
Bouquet Garni (see page 184)
Salt and pepper, to taste

Bone the duck. Preheat oven to 400 degrees.

To prepare stuffing: Melt butter in pan. Add onion and cook until limp but not colored. In a mixing bowl, combine the onions with the ground meat, bread crumbs, parsley, sage, sherry, ham, and pistachio nuts, and mix well. Bind mixture with beaten egg, and season with salt and pepper. Stuff the duck and sew it up neatly with a trussing needle and string, tying at 1- to 2-inch intervals.

Heat oil in roasting pan. Set duck on rack in the roasting pan and baste with hot oil. Roast duck 1¼ hours to 1½ hours in oven, basting every 20 minutes. Turn the bird after 40 minutes.

Meanwhile, make the sauce. Heat oil in pan. Add carrots, onion, and celery, cooking until soft but not colored. Stir in flour and cook slowly until a soft, rich brown color is achieved. Remove pan from heat and stir in 1 cup of the stock and all remaining sauce ingredients, except the remaining chicken stock. Return to heat and stir until sauce boils. Then, simmer very slowly and gently with lid on for 20 to 30 minutes. Add ½ the remaining stock and skim the sauce well. Simmer 5 minutes. Add the rest of the stock and skim again. Simmer for 5 minutes more and strain.

Cook mushrooms in butter until soft. Remove duck from roasting pan and deglaze with sherry. Add strained sauce to the cooked mushrooms.

Serve the duck whole or sliced. If you serve it sliced, pour a little of the sauce over the duck and put the rest of the sauce in a sauceboat on the table. Since duck is a rich meat, it is best served with simple vegetables. Serve with boiled potatoes (little new potatoes are preferred), and another vegetable, such as Braised Celery (see page 157).

SERVES 4.

❦ Miss Jean's Old-Fashioned Southern-Style Chicken and Dumplings

2 whole fryers
2 gallons water
Salt and freshly ground black pepper, to taste
4 cups self-rising flour
¾ cup shortening (we prefer Crisco)
1 cup ice water
2 tablespoons chicken base or chicken-flavored bouillon by Knorr

Place the fryers, water, salt, and pepper into a large pot. Boil until the chicken is tender. Remove the chicken from the pot, and place in a pan to cool. Remove the meat from the bones in large pieces, being careful to remove all dark spots. Set aside.

In a large bowl, mix the flour and shortening together by hand, until the mixture crumbles. Gradually add 1 cup of very cold water until well-mixed. The dough will be stiff. Knead until the dough is "rubbery." On a floured board, roll the dough very thin and cut into 1-inch strips. Drop the dough into the boiling stock. Cook until the dough is done, about 15 minutes.

Add the chicken to the pot with the dumplings, and remove from heat. Do not overcook or the dumplings will be mushy. At this point, it will seem very soupy but, as it will thicken as it sets.

Taste for seasoning at this time. Add more salt and pepper if desired.

Some people like my dumplings served over rice. Serve in bowls along with vegetables and green salad.

SERVES 8 TO 10.

❦ Chicken with Sauce Piquanté

2 chickens (3½ pounds each), cut into pieces
Salt, freshly ground black pepper, and cayenne pepper, to taste
1 cup cooking oil
2 cups onions, chopped
1 cup celery, chopped
1 cup bell pepper, chopped
1 can (16 ounces) whole tomatoes
1 can (16 ounces) tomato juice
5 cups water
1 can (4 ounces) mushrooms
1 tablespoon chicken base or chicken-flavored bouillon by Knorr
1 teaspoon sugar
4 cloves garlic, finely chopped
½ cup green onion tops and bottoms, chopped
¼ cup fresh parsley, chopped

Season the chicken with salt and pepper. In a large saucepan, heat the cooking oil. Fry the chicken in the hot oil until brown. Cover and cook for about 30 minutes, or until the chicken is tender. Take the chicken out and set aside. Add the onion, celery, and bell peppers to the oil that the chicken was cooked in and cook slowly until the onion is tender. Add the tomatoes, tomato juice, and water. Cook over medium heat until oil floats above the tomatoes (about 25 minutes). Add the chicken, mushrooms, chicken base, sugar, and fresh garlic. Season to taste with salt, pepper, and cayenne (piquanté means spicy, so you might want to add a little extra cayenne). Add green onion and parsley. Cook 20 minutes.

Serve over steamed rice.

SERVES 8 TO 10.

❦ Chef Mason's Chicken Clemenceau

1 fresh fryer (3½ pounds), cut into quarters
¼ cup cooking oil
Salt and pepper, to taste
2 baking potatoes, diced
1½ pounds green peas (fresh or frozen — do not use canned peas)
½ pound mushrooms
2 tablespoons garlic, minced
¼ cup butter or margarine
½ cup drippings from chicken

Brush the chicken with oil on both sides, and salt and pepper to taste. Place chicken into a baking dish and cook at 350 degrees until tender and brown (approximately 45 minutes).

In a heavy iron skillet, fry the potatoes in cooking oil over medium heat for 20 to 30 minutes, or until golden-brown and crispy. Drain on a paper towel, and set aside.

Meanwhile, cook the green peas lightly. Be sure not to overcook.

Sauté the mushrooms and garlic in butter until the mushrooms are tender. Add the peas to the mushrooms, and salt and pepper to taste. Add the chicken drippings to the peas and mushrooms. Remove from heat and add the potatoes. Stir lightly.

Place the chicken on a platter or onto individual plates and spoon the peas and mushrooms over the top.

SERVES 4 TO 5.

This is a very old New Orleans dish. It is still on the menus of some very old and famous restaurants.

A tasty variation calls for fresh peeled and deveined shrimp sautéed with salt and pepper just before serving.

❦ Chicken Bonne Femme

1 fresh fryer (3½ pounds), cut into quarters
½ cup cooking oil
Salt and pepper, to taste
⅔ pound bacon, cut into 1-inch slices (thick-sliced bacon is best)
3 large baking potatoes, peeled and sliced
Tony's creole seasoning or Lawry's seasoned salt, to taste
3 large onions, sliced
3 tablespoons cooking oil
1 tablespoon garlic, finely chopped (or more, if desired)
3 teaspoons chicken base or chicken-flavored bouillon by Knorr
½ cup drippings from the chicken

Brush the chicken with oil on both sides, and salt and pepper to taste. Place the chicken in a baking dish and cook at 350 degrees until tender and brown (approximately 45 minutes).

Drain drippings from chicken and add chicken base or bouillon. Pour back over chicken.

Fry the bacon until crisp and brown, and set aside.

In a heavy iron skillet, fry the potatoes in cooking oil for 20 to 30 minutes, or until golden-brown and crispy. Drain on a paper towel, sprinkle lightly with creole seasoning, and set aside.

Meanwhile, sauté the onions in 3 tablespoons oil until tender. Add the garlic and bacon, and cook over low heat for 5 minutes. Add the drippings from the chicken and the potatoes, and stir lightly. Remove from heat.

Place the chicken on a platter or individual plates and spoon the mixture over the chicken.

Serve with a nice green salad and french bread.

SERVES 4.

This recipe was given to me by my very dear friend, Katherine Barras. It was passed along to her by her father-in-law, Chef Josef, chef and manager of Arnaud's Restaurant for 20 years under the previous owner, the late Germaine Wells. This very tasty dish became extremely popular in the '30s, and it is still a great favorite of native New Orleanians and out-of-town visitors alike.

❦ Sautéed Quail

12 semi-boneless quail (split but leave the skin intact)
2 cups flour
½ teaspoon black pepper
½ teaspoon white pepper
½ teaspoon Lawry's seasoned salt
1 tablespoon margarine

Make a seasoned flour and dredge the quail lightly. Add a small amount of butter or margarine to a heavy skillet. Sauté the quail until brown and tender.

Serve on a preheated platter with Brown Butter Sauce (see page 185). Sautéed Quail is delicious served with wild rice and a green vegetable.

SERVES 6.

❦ Stewed Chicken with Mushrooms

1 chicken (3½ to 4 pounds)
Salt and pepper, to taste
1½ cups flour
1 cup cooking oil
½ cup butter or margarine
2 bunches green onions, chopped
1 pound fresh mushrooms, chopped (½ a large can of mushrooms may be substituted)
2 cloves fresh garlic, minced
1 tablespoon chicken base or chicken-flavored bouillon by Knorr
4 cups chicken stock
Steamed rice

Cut the chicken into pieces. Season the chicken with salt and pepper, and roll in flour. In a large saucepan, heat the cooking oil. Cook the chicken in the hot oil until golden-brown on both sides.

While the chicken is cooking, melt the butter or margarine in another large saucepan. Add the onions, mushrooms, garlic, chicken base, and chicken stock. This will be the gravy. Add the chicken to the pan and cook for 25 minutes over very low heat, or place in a Pyrex baking pan in a 350-degree oven until the chicken is tender.

Serve over steamed rice.

SERVES 4.

❦ *Oyster Dressing*

5 dozen small oysters with their liquor
1 loaf French bread (the wide type)
½ stick butter or margarine
Turkey giblets, finely chopped
2 medium onions, finely chopped
3 stalks celery, finely chopped
1 bell pepper, finely chopped
3 medium cloves garlic, finely chopped
4 sprigs parsley, finely chopped
4 green onions, finely chopped
1 bay leaf
¼ teaspoon thyme

Remove the shell pieces from the oysters if there are any. Poach the oysters in their own liquor (about 2 cups; add water to make this amount) for about 5 minutes. Remove the oysters and chop them coarsely. Break the bread into small pieces and soak in the oyster liquor. Melt the butter in a large skillet or sauté pan; add the giblets, onion, celery and bell pepper, and cook until tender. Then, add the garlic, parsley, and green onions, and sauté briefly. Add bay leaves and thyme. Add the oysters and cook a short while before adding the soaked bread. Place in an open dish and bake in a 300-degree oven for about 30 minutes.

Serve with turkey and Giblet Gravy (see page 179).

❦ Cornbread Dressing

½ stick butter or margarine
1 cup celery, chopped
1 cup onions, chopped
3 cups cornbread crumbs
1½ cups bread cubes (day-old bread)
1 teaspoon sage
1 teaspoon poultry seasoning
Salt and freshly ground black pepper, to taste
1 tablespoon chicken base or chicken-flavored bouillon cubes by Knorr
4 cups chicken stock

Sauté the celery and onion in the butter in a skillet until limp but not browned. In a large bowl, mix the cornbread crumbs, bread cubes, sage, poultry seasoning, salt, and pepper. Add chicken base. Add the onion, celery, and chicken stock, and mix well. Bake in a 1½-quart casserole at 350 degrees until golden-brown.

SERVES 8 OR ENOUGH FOR A 10-POUND TURKEY.

This dressing is excellent when served with turkey, chicken, pork, or veal.

SEAFOOD

❦ *Creole Crawfish Etoufee*

1 cup butter or margarine (better if ½ butter and ½ margarine)
1 cup white onions, finely chopped
½ cup celery, finely chopped
1 cup green onions, finely chopped
2 teaspoons minced garlic
3 tablespoons flour
1 cup tomatoes, peeled and chopped fine
2 cups Chicken Stock (see page 187)
1 teaspoon salt
1 teaspoon freshly ground black pepper
1 tablespoon Worcestershire sauce (we prefer Lea & Perrin's)
1½ cup crawfish tails
¼ teaspoon cayenne pepper
1 cup cooked white rice

In a large heavy saucepan, melt the butter and margarine, and add the onion, celery. and green onions. Sauté over medium heat until tender. Add the garlic and continue cooking for 1 minute. Gradually add the flour, stirring constantly until golden-brown. Then, add the tomatoes and cook for 5 minutes before adding the Chicken Stock, salt, pepper, cayenne, Worcestershire sauce, and crawfish tails. Cook over low heat for 15 to 20 minutes.

To serve, mound ½ cup of rice in the center of a deep plate or soup bowl and surround with Crawfish Etoufee.

SERVES 4 TO 6.

This is one of the most popular creole dishes that we serve at Miss Ruby's Restaurant. Shrimp may be substituted for the crawfish.

🍂 Basic Fried or Broiled Trout

1 cup all-purpose four
1 teaspoon salt
½ teaspoon white pepper
½ teaspoon freshly ground black pepper
1 teaspoon creole seasoning (we prefer Tony's)
½ teaspoon Lawry's seasoned salt
2 eggs
1 cup milk
1 cup peanut oil (we prefer Louana)
6 skinless speckled trout fillets (6 ounces each)
2 lemons, wedged

Place flour in a mixing bowl and add salt, white pepper, black pepper, creole seasoning, and Lawry's seasoned salt. Stir well and set aside. Make egg wash in another bowl by beating eggs with a wire whisk and mixing in milk.

To fry the trout: Heat oil to 375 degrees in a deep-fat fryer or deep skillet. If you use a skillet, put in only enough oil to come over the sides of the fish. Dredge the fillets in the seasoned flour, dip in the egg wash and back in the flour. Cook in the oil until golden-brown. Serve the trout on a heated plate and garnish with lemon wedges and fresh parsley or watercress.

To broil the trout: Place the fillets in a Pyrex baking dish, and sprinkle lightly with Lawry's seasoned salt, white pepper, and paprika. Dot with butter and bake in a 325-degree oven until the fish turns white or becomes tender. Baste and run under the broiler briefly to brown.

Serve piping hot with parsleyed new potatoes or Oven-Browned Potatoes (see page 152) and a green vegetable.

SERVES 6.

These can be used to create Trout Almondine (see page 140), Trout Eugene (see page 125), and Trout Meuniere (see page 140). For best results, always use fresh seafood.

❧ Rod's Smoked Salmon

1. Make a smoked salmon brine using:
   2 quarts water
   ½ cup noniodized salt
   1½ cups brown sugar
   1 teaspoon garlic powder
   2 tablespoons soy sauce
   1 teaspoon freshly ground black pepper
   1 teaspoon Worcestershire sauce (we prefer Lea & Perrin's)
   1 bottle Johnny's Seafood Seasoning (or any good seafood seasoning)

   Cut a small salmon (8 pounds or more) into serving-sized pieces and fillet. Place them in a large glass bowl and cover with the brine. Refrigerate overnight. The next day, remove from the brine and allow to dry at room temperature for about 1 hour.

2. If the fillets are 1 inch thick or larger:
   Pre-cook by baking in a 325-degree oven for 15 to 20 minutes to cut the smoking time dramatically.

3. Smoke over Alderwood chips for 5 to 6 hours for the best salmon you ever tasted. (We recommend a "Little Chief Smoker" made in Hood River, Oregon, by Jenson.) Smoked Salmon may be refrigerated for 2 weeks, and keeps well frozen for 6 months. Any firm fish can be smoked and enjoyed.

   This recipe was given to me by my youngest son, Rod Smart, who lives in Rochester, Washington. Rod is an avid salmon fisherman, and his friends are always asking what he uses for bait. His secret is crawfish tails, which I send to him frozen in water. It seems both salmon and steelheads can't get enough of our Louisiana delicacy.

❦ *Shrimp Diane*

8 tablespoons margarine
2 tablespoons flour
1 cup milk
1 cup evaporated milk
2 cups Chicken Stock (see page 187)
1 teaspoon garlic, minced
½ teaspoon garlic powder
1 teaspoon onion powder
¼ teaspoon oregano
½ teaspoon thyme
1 teaspoon Lawry's seasoned salt (or to taste), divided
½ teaspoon white pepper
¼ teaspoon freshly ground black pepper
½ teaspoon sage (optional)
¼ teaspoon cayenne pepper
2 tablespoons chicken base or chicken bouillon cubes by Knorr
2 pounds large shrimp, peeled and deveined, with tails
5 quarts boiling water
1 package (16 ounces) enriched egg noodles
1 teaspoon salt
1 bunch green onions, finely sliced
½ cup fresh mushrooms, sliced
2 tablespoons white wine

Melt 4 tablespoons margarine in a large, heavy saucepan and add the flour to make a medium-brown Roux (see page 181). Then, add the milk and the Chicken Stock, and cook, stirring constantly, over medium heat until it begins to thicken to a light sauce. Add the garlic, garlic powder, onion powder, oregano, thyme, ½ teaspoon Lawry's seasoned salt, white pepper, black pepper, sage, cayenne pepper, and chicken base. Cook over low heat for 10 minutes and set aside.

In a large, heavy skillet melt 3 tablespoons of butter and add the shrimp. Season with ½ teaspoon of Lawry's seasoned salt and cook over medium heat until they begin to turn pink. Then, add all the sauce to the shrimp pan and cook over low heat for 3 minutes.

Boil 5 quarts of salted water in a large saucepan, add the egg noodles, and cook until done. Drain in a colander and rinse with very hot water, then cold water, to stop the cooking process. Pour 1 tablespoon of melted butter in the noodles and mix carefully to prevent them from sticking together.

Slice the tops and bottoms of one bunch of green onions and place them in a small bowl to be used as fresh garnish. In a separate small skillet, melt 2 tablespoons butter and sauté the sliced mushrooms for 3 minutes. Add the white wine and keep warm until ready to serve.

Divide the pasta among four warmed plates and spoon the hot shrimp mixture over the noodles. Top with sautéed mushrooms in wine sauce and sprinkle with finely sliced green onions.

SERVES 4.

Over the years, our customers have told us how much they appreciate the fine quality of the food we serve. We always use the best and freshest ingredients available. The other thing we do is recreate some of the old favorites like Shrimp Diane which was very popular in the 1950s and early '60s. It is still one of the very best shrimp dishes, originated here in New Orleans by one of our talented chefs.

❦ *Trout Eugene*

To prepare, use the Basic Fried or Broiled Trout (see page 122) and our famous Crabmeat Topping (see page 131).

For garnish, fry or broil 12 medium peeled and deveined shrimp (with tails) with the trout fillets. Lay two shrimp on crabmeat topping before serving. Add two wedges of lemon and fresh parsley or watercress.

Trout Eugene is one of the most popular dishes we serve at Miss Ruby's Restaurant. It is not only pretty to look at, but it is truly a delight for the palate, too.

❦ Catfish Bordelaise

8 catfish fillets (4 to 5 ounces each)
4 teaspoons virgin olive oil
4 teaspoons garlic, minced
2 tablespoons fresh parsley, freshly chopped
Lawry's seasoned salt, to taste
½ teaspoon paprika

Roll each fillet in the olive oil to coat and then pat a mixture of the garlic, parsley, Lawry's seasoned salt, and paprika on all sides of each fillet. Lay the seasoned fish in a Pyrex baking dish and bake in a 350-degree oven until tender. To microwave, cover with plastic wrap and cook two at a time for about 4 minutes. Do not overcook.
   Serve with fluffy white rice and a green vegetable.

SERVES 4.

This is one of my favorite ways to cook catfish. We buy farm-raised catfish. I have personally been to the farms in Mississippi's delta country. The fish are fed on grain made from corn and soybean meal, which make the fish high in protein. The plants where the fish are processed are as clean as an operating room. The workers wear white uniforms and keep their heads covered, and the fish are never touched by bare hands.

❦ Fried Catfish

8 catfish fillets (5 ounces each)
2 cups white corn meal
1 teaspoon creole seasoning (we prefer Tony's)
½ teaspoon Lawry's seasoned salt
1 teaspoon freshly ground black pepper
2 eggs, beaten
1 cup milk
2 cups peanut oil

Mix the cornmeal with Lawry's seasoned salt, creole seasoning, and pepper in an open bowl. Wash the fish fillets and pat dry. Beat the eggs and milk in a separate bowl with a wire whisk to make the "egg wash." Heat the peanut oil to 325 degrees in a deep-fat fryer or, with the skillet method, use enough oil to come up to the sides of the fillets. Dip each fillet in the egg wash and dredge with cornmeal. Cook until golden-brown and crispy on both sides (3 to 5 minutes).

Serve with Hush Puppies (see page 195), French fries, Coleslaw (see page 69), and Miss Jean's Tartar Sauce (see page 180).

SERVES 4.

❦ *Broiled Catfish*

4 tablespoons margarine, melted
1 teaspoon Lawry's seasoned salt
½ teaspoon white pepper
¼ teaspoon paprika
8 catfish fillets (3 to 4 ounces each)
1 tablespoon water

Season the fish with Lawry's seasoned salt and white pepper. Place the fillets in a baking dish and sprinkle with a little paprika. Drizzle the melted margarine over the fish and add the water to the bottom of the pan. Bake in a 350-degree oven for 10 minutes and then run under the broiler to brown.

Serve with a mound of white rice and spoon a little of the stock from the baking dish over the fish and rice. This dish is always good with a green salad and vegetable.

SERVES 4.

❦ Blackened Redfish

4 redfish fillets (8 ounces each), or any firm white fish
1 stick margarine
Blackened Seasoning (see page 3)

Melt margarine in a large cast iron skillet over high heat. While the skillet is heating, sprinkle the fish fillets with the Blackened Seasoning on both sides. Cook for about 5 minutes on each side. Test for fork tenderness. If the fish seems to be browning too fast, lower the heat to assure that the center is done.

Serve with Oven-Browned Potatoes (see page 152) and a green vegetable.

SERVES 4.

This is the dish Paul Prudehomme made so famous, and is always one of the most popular dishes at Miss Ruby's. You will need a commercial vent over your stove, or plan to cook on an outdoor burner, because a great deal of smoke is created while preparing this tasty dish.

❦ Broiled Redfish

4 redfish fillets (8 ounces each), red snapper or any firm white fish
1 teaspoon Lawry's seasoned salt
1 teaspoon freshly ground black pepper
½ teaspoon white pepper
½ teaspoon creole seasoning (we recommend Tony's)
½ teaspoon paprika
¼ pound butter or margarine, melted
2 tablespoons water

Put the Lawry's seasoned salt, black pepper, white pepper, and creole seasoning in a mixing bowl and stir. Wash fish fillets, place in an open baking dish (individual dishes are nice if you have them), and rub well with the seasoning mixture. Pour the melted butter on and around the fish, and add the water to the pan. Run under the broiler and cook about 10 minutes or until tender, or place in a pan on the bottom rack of a 400-degree oven for 15 minutes. Baste the fish at least once while it is cooking.

Serve with a mound of fluffy white rice. Pour a little of the broth from the pan over the rice. This dish is good when served with green vegetables and a crisp green salad.

SERVES 4.

❦ Ruby's Shrimp

3 tablespoons olive oil
28 large shrimp, peeled and deveined, with tails
¼ cup butter
2 small cloves garlic, minced
¼ teaspoon Lawry's seasoned salt
¼ teaspoon freshly ground black pepper
Dash cayenne pepper (if you like things spicy)
¼ cup dry vermouth
3 tablespoons lemon juice

Put the olive oil in a large skillet over a medium heat and add the shrimp. Cook until golden-brown and turn. Reduce the heat and add the butter, garlic, salt, and pepper. When this is all well-blended, raise the heat to high and add the vermouth and lemon juice. Stir or shake the skillet constantly for 1 minute.

SERVES 6 AS AN APPETIZER OR 4 AS A MAIN COURSE.

We are so fortunate to have our wonderful fresh shrimp here in New Orleans and this is a fantastic way to prepare them. Vermouth was first used in cooking during World War II when wines were scarce. Use dry vermouth in recipes that call for wine and you will notice the improvement in the bouquet and flavor. Try some over your steaks also. It will make a little au-jus right on your plate.

❦ Oysters Joseph

½ cup green onions, chopped
½ cup butter
4 dozen oysters and liquor
Dash Tabasco
Salt and freshly ground black pepper, to taste
½ cup unseasoned bread crumbs
¼ cup Parmesan cheese, grated

In a large heavy skillet, sauté the green onions in butter until they are soft. Add the oysters, oyster liquor, and seasonings. Simmer 15 minutes and pour into a greased baking dish or individual ramekins. Sprinkle with a mixture of bread crumbs and Parmesan cheese. Dot with butter and broil for about 3 minutes or until the topping browns.

SERVES 4 AS AN ENTRÉE OR 8 AS AN APPETIZER.

This recipe was given to me by Alfred Sunsere, president of P&J Oyster Company in New Orleans, where we can always depend on finding the best and freshest oysters. When I go to buy my osyers for Miss Ruby's Restaurant, the oyster shuckers are always busy.

❦ Crabmeat au Gratin

¼ cup butter or margarine
¼ cup bell pepper, finely diced
¼ cup celery, finely diced
¼ cup green onion, diced
⅓ cup instantized flour (we recommend Gold Medal Wondra)
1½ cups milk
1 teaspoon fresh parsley, finely chopped
Salt and cayenne pepper, to taste
1 teaspoon garlic powder
1 pound fancy lump crabmeat
¼ pound mild cheddar cheese, grated

Melt the butter in a heavy skillet over medium heat. Stir in the bell pepper, celery, and onion, and simmer until tender. Sprinkle the flour over the cooked vegetables and stir until smooth and bubbling lightly. Add the milk slowly while stirring constantly until thickened (3 to 4 minutes). Then, add the parsley, salt, pepper, and garlic. Reserve ¼ of the cheese for garnish and add the majority to the mixture. Stir until melted. Remove the sauce from the heat and gently fold in the crabmeat. Pour into a 1-quart casserole and garnish with cheese and paprika. Bake in a 375-degree oven for 5 minutes or until the cheese is melted and bubbly.

SERVES 6.

This dish may be divided among individual ramekins to serve the same number of people.

This recipe was given to me by my good friend Carolyn Lestremau Scanlin. It is an old family recipe that we tested in our kitchen and have continued to serve ever since. It's a real favorite!

❦ Lump Crabmeat Topping

1½ sticks butter or margarine
1 bunch green onions, finely sliced
¼ teaspoon white pepper
¼ teaspoon Lawry's seasoned salt
1 clove garlic, minced
1 pound fancy lump crabmeat

Melt the butter in a heavy saucepan or skillet and sauté the green onion and garlic for about 3 minutes (do not let the onion brown). Add the salt, pepper, and crabmeat, and shake the pan lightly to stir. Do not break the lumps apart. Keep warm.

Serve with any dish that calls for crabmeat dressing or topping — Trout Eugene (page 125), Veal Oscar (page 84), Fried or Broiled Fish (page 122), or with fettucini or egg noodles.

🍃 Louisiana's Fried Soft-Shell Crab

4 large soft-shell crabs or 8 small ones
2 cups all-purpose flour
1 teaspoon creole seasoning (we prefer Tony's)
½ teaspoon Lawry's seasoned salt
1 teaspoon freshly ground black pepper
2 eggs
1½ cups milk
1 quart peanut oil (or more if deep-frying, which is preferable)

Clean the crabs by lifting the top shell at both end points and scraping the gills (or "dead man") out with a paring knife. Then, use kitchen sissors and cut off the mouth and eyes. Turn the crab over, lift the flap and cut it off. Now, wash the crabs well under cold running water, being careful not to break off any of the legs or claws. Set aside to drain.

In a large bowl, mix the flour, creole seasoning, Lawry's seasoned salt, and black pepper. Beat the eggs in another bowl with a wire whisk and add the milk to make an "egg wash." Heat the peanut oil in a deep-fat fryer to 375 degrees. The crabs must have space to float on the surface and spread their legs out. Dredge the crabs in the flour mixture, one at a time, dip in the egg wash, and back in the flour. Be sure they are well-coated. Place in the hot oil one or two at a time, depending on the size of the fryer. Cook until they surface and, then, turn them over to brown evenly on both sides and to ensure the body parts are cooked through.

Serve on a heated plate with French fries or Oven-Browned Potatoes (see page 152) and a green vegetable.

SERVES 4.

In Louisiana, soft-shell crabs are farmed because they must be caught at the time they shed their hard shell. Battestillas Seafood delivers live crabs daily when they are in season, so we know they are fresh. Any not used that day are wrapped individually in plastic wrap and frozen for later use. Crab will keep frozen for 2 to 3 weeks. Crab is high in protein, low in fat, and rich in minerals.

❦ *Louisiana-Style Boiled Shrimp*

4 yellow onions, quartered
1 whole head fresh garlic, cut in half crossways
1 bunch celery, cut in pieces
9 bay leaves
Salt to taste (about ½ cup because most of the salt stays in the water)
3 tablespoons cayenne pepper
2 tablespoons black pepper
4 lemons, sliced
2 bags of crab boil (we prefer Zatarain's)
5 pounds shrimp (with heads on preferred)

Fill a large pot with two gallons of water. Place all of the above ingredients, except crab boil and shrimp, in the pot of water and boil for 1 hour. Add two bags of crab boil for the last 25 minutes.

Add shrimp and bring to a boil for 3 to 5 minutes (boiling time depends on the size of the shrimp). Test for doneness and seasoning. Remove pot from the stove. Pour cold water on top of the shrimp or ice down and allow to stand for about 10 minutes tol help the shrimp absorb the spices. Drain the shrimp in a colander and spread on a large pan to cool.

SERVES 10 TO 12 AS AN APPETIZER.

In Louisiana where we have an abundance of fresh shrimp, it's quite popular to have "shrimp boils" where guests peel and dip their own. The host should provide bowls of Remoulade Sauce (see page 186) or Red Cocktail Sauce (see page 183).

❦ Oyster Loaf

1 tablespoon creole seasoning (we prefer Tony's)
½ teaspoon Lawry's seasoned salt
1 teaspoon freshly ground black pepper
½ gallon shucked oysters in their own liquor
1½ cups white cornmeal
1½ cups all-purpose flour
2 cups peanut oil (we prefer Louana)

Mix the creole seasoning, Lawry's seasoned salt, and black pepper in a small bowl. Place the oysters and their liquor in a bowl and sprinkle half of the seasoning over them. Mix in well and set aside. Put the cornmeal and the flour in a large bowl with the other half of the seasoning and mix well. Heat peanut oil in a deep-fat fryer or deep skillet to 375 degrees. Lift seasoned oysters out of the bowl with a slotted spoon and drain slightly. Dredge in seasoned flour-cornmeal mixture and cook a few at a time for 1½ to 2 minutes — *no longer,* because you want the oysters to be tasty.

Spread Garlic Mayonnaise (see page 178) on a 10-inch piece of toasted French bread which has been cut in half and crowd the oysters on one half.

To make a "dressed" oyster loaf or po-boy, top with sliced tomatoes and shredded lettuce.

SERVES 4 TO 6.

Oysters fried in this manner may also be served as a main course with french fries and a green salad. Serves 8 to 10 according to size and appetite with Tartar Sauce (see page 180) or Red Cocktail Sauce (see page 183).

Be sure to feel each oyster for bits of shell or hard muscle before cooking. This is called "feeling the oysters."

❦ Sautéed Redfish

1½ sticks butter or margarine
6 green onions, sliced
½ pound fancy lump crabmeat
1 teaspoon Lawry's seasoned salt
¼ teaspoon white pepper
1½ cups flour
½ teaspoon salt
½ teaspoon creole seasoning (we prefer Tony's)
½ teaspoon freshly ground black pepper
4 redfish fillets (8 to 10 ounces each) (red snapper or trout may be used)
½ cup Hollandaise Sauce (see page 187)
1 cup Brown Butter Sauce (see page 185)

Melt a stick of butter in a medium saucepan over medium heat. Add the onions and sauté lightly before adding the lump crabmeat. Sprinkle with ¼ teaspoon Lawry's seasoned salt and ¼ teaspoon white pepper. Warm and set aside to use as topping. Be careful not to break the lumps apart.

Place the flour in a large bowl and add the salt, Lawry's seasoned salt, creole seasoning, and black pepper. Mix well and set aside. To cook all four fillets at once, use two large heavy skillets and melt half a stick of butter in each over medium heat. Dredge the fillets in the flour mixture and cook until golden-brown.

To serve, put 2 tablespoons Brown Butter Sauce on a preheated plate and place the fillet in the center. Put one-quarter of the crabmeat mixture on top of each fillet and top with a tablespoon of Hollandaise Sauce. Serve with parsleyed potatoes or Oven-Browned Potatoes (see page 152).

SERVES 4.

❦ Boiled Crawfish

20 pounds live crawfish
¼ cup salt, or more to taste
1 jar seafood boil in granulated form (Cajun Land)
4 lemons, cut in half
4 whole heads of garlic, cut in half crosswise
2 pounds whole new potatoes
2 ounces liquid crab boil
1 head celery, cut into 4-inch lengths
4 ears fresh corn, cut into 3 pieces each
3 trays of ice

Purge the crawfish by putting them into a large tub, cover with cold water and add the salt. Gently stir the salt into the the water. Soak for 20 minutes and then rinse. You can use the bathtub so that the water may easily be drained.

Fill a very large pot with water, and add the seafood boil, lemons, garlic and potatoes. Bring to a boil and allow to boil for 10 minutes. Add the crab boil. Then add the live crawfish, corn and celery. Boil 5 minutes on high heat. Turn off the heat. Test for texture and doneness. Add the ice cubes to the crawfish. The crawfish will sink to the bottom. Leave them in the pot for approximately 10 minutes. Do not over cook or they will be very hard to peel. Drain and spread on newspaper. Peel and enjoy. Crawfish are best when served hot.

When crawfish come into season in the early spring, the people of Louisiana know winter is over. These small freshwater crustaceans, relatives of the lobster, are an integral part of both Cajun and Creole cuisine. The crawfish is farm-raised about nine months of the year. But in the spring, when they can be caught in the bayous, rivers and lakes, crawfish boils are held all across Louisiana. A crawfish boil is indeed a day of fun, with friends gathering and, of course, Cajun music and dancing.

❦ Shrimp Remoulade

3 pounds shrimp (for an appetizer, figure on 8 to 10 shrimp per person,
    depending on size of shrimp)
Remoulade Sauce (see page 186)
1 head Romaine or Boston lettuce
1 head iceberg lettuce

Boil shrimp; peel and devein. Place shrimp in bowl, and cover with
Remoulade Sauce. Stir until all shrimp are well-covered; refrigerate for 1
hour or more.

Line a salad plate with Romaine lettuce (or any other pretty, curly lettuce). Fill the center of the plate with shredded iceberg lettuce, and place
the shrimp mixture on top.

❦ Shrimp Scampi

1 stick margarine
1½ pounds large shrimp, peeled and deveined
2 teaspoons chopped garlic
6 fresh onions chopped
3 cups Bechemel or White Wine Sauce (see page 183)
1 teaspoon Lawry's seasoned salt
1 pound egg noodles

Melt margarine in a heavy skillet. Sauté shrimp until pink. Add garlic,
Lawry's seasoned salt, and green onions. To this mixture, add White Wine
Sauce and cook 3 minutes.

Cook egg noodles in 5 quarts of boiling water with ½ teaspoon of salt
until tender (to keep the pasta from sticking together, add a tablespoon of
olive oil to the water, or, after draining the pasta, work the olive oil
through the noodles). Wash and drain noodles well.

Place noodles on a serving plate and arrange shrimp mixture on top.
Sprinkle with green onions.

SERVES 4.

❧ Stuffed Shrimp

2 dozen large shrimp, peeled and deveined, with tails

EGG WASH
3 eggs
⅓ can Pet milk
2 cups water

STUFFING
1 stick margarine
1 cup onion, finely chopped
1 cup green onion, thinly sliced (tops and bottoms)
¾ cup green bell pepper, finely chopped
1 cup celery, finely chopped
3 tablespoons garlic, minced
3 tablespoons parsley, chopped
1 teaspoon garlic powder
1 teaspoon onion powder
1 teaspoon Lawry's seasoned salt
1 teaspoon ground sage
1 teaspoon ground thyme
1 teaspoon black pepper
1 teaspoon white pepper
1 teaspoon cayenne pepper
3 cups bread crumbs
1 cup evaporated milk
1 pound crabmeat, white or claw meat
2 pounds shrimp, chopped
1 teaspoon chicken base or bouillon granules

Sauté onion, green pepper, celery, garlic and parsley in the margarine until limp. Then, add all remaining stuffing ingredients except chopped shrimp and crabmeat. Continue cooking for 20 minutes. Add crabmeat and shrimp, and cook until shrimp turns pink. Remove from heat, place in a large bowl, and cool.

Spread the whole shrimp on a platter open side up. Place approximately 1 ounce of the stuffing on each shrimp and press the stuffing in and around the shrimp to make a nice fat shrimp shape (at this point the shrimp may be frozen). Make an egg wash by combining the eggs, Pet milk, and water. Dip shrimp into egg wash, roll in flour, then dip into egg wash again, finally rolling shrimp in unseasoned bread crumbs. Deep-fat-fry, or fry in a heavy skillet with enough oil to cover the shrimp, at 350 degrees for approximately 15 minutes.

❦ New Orleans Famous Bar-B-Que Shrimp

1 pound large fresh shrimp, with heads (16 to 20 count is best)
¼ cup water
½ cup butter or margarine
4 cloves garlic, minced
2 tablespoons freshly ground black pepper
½ teaspoons paprika
¼ teaspoon cayenne

Wash the shrimp well and drain. Add the water. Melt the butter in an open baking dish or pan, and lay the shrimp in the butter. Sprinkle the seasonings and garlic over the shrimp. Place a baking dish on the bottom of a very hot oven (450 degrees). When the shrimp start to cook, turn over with a spatula and return to high heat. Cook no more than 15 minutes.
Serve with bibs and hot French bread to dip in the juice.

SERVES 2.

For a variation, add 1 teaspoon Worcestershire sauce.

❦ Chef Mason's
Trout Meuniere Sauce

½ pound butter
¼ cup Worcestershire sauce (we prefer Lea & Perrin's)
2 lemons, juiced

Combine all ingredients in a heavy skillet or saucepan with half a lemon that has been squeezed. Cook over medium heat until the butter clarifies and the sauce is slightly brown. Reduce heat to warm and allow the sauce to sit while you prepare Basic Fried or Broiled Trout (see page 122).

❦ Basic Almondine Sauce

1 cup sliced almonds
1 teaspoon butter or margarine

Spread the almonds on a cookie sheet and bake in a 350-degree oven until lightly browned. Melt butter in a small skillet and stir in almonds to lightly oil. Sprinkle over Basic Fried or Broiled Trout fillets (see page 122).

JAMBALAYAS

❦ *Joann's Shrimp Jambalaya*

½ pound thick-sliced bacon, cut in pieces
½ pound creole smoked sausage or any good-quality Polish sausage, thinly
   sliced
3 large onions, finely chopped
1 bell pepper, finely chopped
½ bunch parsley, chopped very finely
3 large cloves garlic, minced
2 bay leaves, crushed
½ teaspoon thyme
1 teaspoon salt
⅛ teaspoon cayenne pepper
1 pound medium shrimp, peeled and deveined
1½ cups white rice
3 cups water
1 can (6 ounces) tomato sauce (we prefer Hunt's)

In a large skillet, cook the bacon until it is crisp. Remove, blot with paper towels, and set aside. Drain off and reserve the bacon grease. In the same skillet, fry the sausage until slightly browned. Remove and drain. Leave 2 tablespoons of the sausage grease in the skillet and add 1 tablesppon of the bacon drippings. Put the skillet on medium heat, add the onions and bell pepper, and cook until tender. Add the parsley, sausage, bacon, garlic, and seasonings, and mix well. Lay the shrimp on top and pour the uncooked rice over the shrimp. Add water to barely cover the rice and pour the tomato sauce over this. Cover and bring to a boil. Reduce the heat and cook for 30 minutes. Remove the cover, reduce the heat to very low, and cook for 15 minutes to dry out.

SERVES 6 TO 8.

Joann says DO NOT stir. Serve directly from the pan.

❦ Creole Jambalaya with Chicken, Tasso, and Andouille

6 tablespoons margarine
3 cups raw white rice
¾ pound Andouille sausage or any good Polish sausage
¾ pound Tasso or lean smoked ham (we prefer Hormel Cure 81)
1 pound boneless, skinless chicken breasts, or 2 whole chicken breasts
3 bay leaves
3 tablespoons any good spicy creole seasoning mix
1½ cups onion, chopped
1½ cups celery, chopped
1 cup bell pepper, chopped
2 tablespoons garlic, minced
¾ cup tomato sauce
1 cup fresh tomatoes, peeled and chopped
3½ cups Basic Chicken Stock (see page 187)

Melt 3 tablespoons butter in a heavy skillet and add the raw rice. Cook over medium heat until golden-brown, stirring constantly. Chop the sausage, tasso, and chicken breasts into bite-sized pieces. Melt 5 tablespoons of margarine in a heavy 6-quart saucepan or Dutch oven and cook the sausage and Tasso over medium heat until they start to brown. Add the chicken pieces and continue cooking until it browns (about 5 minutes). Put in the bay leaves, creole seasoning, onion, celery, bell pepper, and garlic, and cook until the vegetables become limp (about 10 minutes). Stir in the tomato sauce and cook for 5 minutes before adding the chopped tomatoes. (Be sure to stir often while cooking to prevent sticking.) Add the chicken stock and the browned rice, bring to a boil, and reduce the heat. Simmer, covered, on low heat until the rice is tender (about 20 to 25 minutes). Do not overcook or the rice will become mushy. Remove the bay leaves before serving. If you like it spicy, add more cayenne pepper to taste.

Serve about 1 cup as a main course and ½ cup as an appetizer.

SERVES 10 TO 12.

We serve this at Miss Ruby's with fresh string beans or green peas (not canned), whole kernel corn and a crisp garden salad. Serving the vegetables on either side of the mound of jambalaya makes an attractive dish.

❦ Cajun Crawfish Jambalaya

1 stick butter or margarine
2 cups long grain rice (we suggest Uncle Ben's Converted)
1 cup onions, chopped
½ cup celery, chopped
¼ cup parsley, finely chopped
½ cup green onions, chopped
1 teaspoon fresh garlic, minced
1 teaspoon salt
1½ teaspoons cayenne pepper (or less)
½ teaspoon Tony's creole seasoning
2 teaspoons chicken base or chicken bouillon granules
2 tablespoons Worcestershire sauce
1 pound crawfish tails
4 cups boiling water

Melt the margarine in a heavy pot over medium heat. Add the uncooked rice and stir constantly until the rice becomes golden-brown. Add the onions and green pepper to the rice, and sauté until the vegetables are limp. Add the crawfish tails, salt, creole seasoning, and cayenne pepper, and cook 3 to 5 minutes over medium heat. Stir in the garlic. Then, add the boiling water (it is very important that the water is boiling). Add the green onions, parsley, Worcestershire sauce, and chicken base, and bring to a rolling boil. Reduce heat and cover, cooking slowly for 20 minutes, or until the rice is tender and flaky, but not mushy. Remove from heat and allow to stand at least 5 minutes before serving.

At *Miss Ruby's*, we serve this dish by pressing the jambalaya into a small cup and inverting the cup onto a plate. This makes an attractive mound. We put green peas and whole kernel corn on the plate with the jambalaya and serve a fresh garden salad on the side.

The jambalaya will keep for 2 days in the refrigerator. It can be frozen, but it will lose some of its flavor.

> *This is our recipe that we serve at the famous French Quarter festival each spring in Jackson Square. We use 500 pounds of rice and 200 pounds of crawfish tails, and we can't make it fast enough. We have a very popular booth, with a long line waiting all day. It's a lot of work, but a lot of fun. We get to listen to the world's best jazz bands all day long for 2 days.*

❦ Cajun Jambalaya with Andouille Sausage and Tasso

SEASONING MIX
5 small bay leaves
½ teaspoon salt
1 teaspoon white pepper
1 teaspoon cayenne pepper
½ teaspoon cumin
½ teaspoon black pepper
½ teaspoon dried thyme leaves

5 tablespoons margarine
3 cups white rice, browned (we prefer Uncle Ben's)
½ pound Tasso or other smoked ham (we prefer Hormel Cure 81)
½ pound Andouille smoked sausage or any good polish sausage
2 cups onions, chopped
2 cups celery, chopped
1 cup bell pepper, chopped
2 teaspoons garlic, minced
½ stick margarine
5½ cups Basic Chicken Stock (see page 187)

Combine the seasonings and set aside. In a heavy skillet, melt the margarine and brown the raw rice over medium heat, stirring constantly until golden-brown. Chop the Tasso and Andouille sausage. Melt the margarine in another heavy skillet (cast iron preferred) and cook the Tasso and sausage over high heat for 5 minutes or so. Add the onion, celery, bell pepper, garlic, and seasoning mix, and continue to cook, stirring frequently, until browned (about 10 minutes). Stir in the browned rice and add the stock. Stir well and bring to a boil. Reduce the heat and simmer until the rice is tender but still crunchy (about 20 minutes). This must be stirred frequently to keep the rice from sticking and burning. Remove the bay leaves and serve immediately, or pour into a long flat open pan to cool so it will not continue to cook.

Vegetables

❦ Sweet and Sour Green Beans

3 slices bacon, fried crisp
¼ cup wine vinegar
1½ teaspoons sugar
1 can (16 ounces) whole Blue Lake green beans

Cook the bacon and set it aside. Put the vinegar and sugar into the skillet with the bacon drippings and add enough water or liquid from the beans to cover the bottom of the skillet. Add the drained beans and simmer them for 25 minutes, stirring occasionally. Place in a serving bowl and top with crumbled bacon.

SERVES 4.

This vegetable dish is easy and good.

❦ Ann's Zucchini and Baby Carrots

¾ pound baby carrots
1½ cups water
2 medium zucchini squash, cut in ½-inch slices
¼ teaspoon dried Italian seasonings
¼ teaspoon freshly ground black pepper
½ cube chicken bouillon
2 pats butter
⅛ teaspoon garlic powder
1 lemon

Put the carrots and water into a pot. Cover and cook over medium heat for 5 minutes. Remove from the heat and add remaining ingredients. Mix well. (If this mixture sits for 30 minutes, the vegetables will absorb the seasonings.) Cover and cook for 3 to 5 minutes just before serving. Drain off the water and add the butter.

❦ Joann's Cabbage

1 medium head cabbage
3 tablespoons butter or margarine
3 tablespoons Crisco shortening
Salt and freshly ground black pepper, to taste
½ cup cooked egg noodles (optional)

Cut the cabbage in quarters and remove the core. Then, shred the cabbage medium to fine and set aside. Put the butter and Crisco in a large, heavy skillet (preferably an iron skillet) and place on medium to high heat. When the oil is hot, add all of the cabbage and cover. Let it fry a few minutes before stirring. When you notice that there are a few brown bits, lower the heat and add more butter if needed. If there are a few burned pieces, just pick them out and discard. As you continue to cook the cabbage, add the salt and black pepper, and cook until a little crunchy. Serve just this way or stir in the egg noodles for a very different dish.

SERVES 4.

This is a German/Russian recipe from Joann's great-grandmother which she first prepared for me in Cancun, Mexico. The cabbage at the market there is as pretty as our own creole cabbage and the best I have ever eaten. One of the things that makes this dish so special is that it cooks in its own juice.

❦ Chef Oscar's Creole Okra

Okra is the pod of a tall annual of the mallow family. It was originally cultivated as a thickening agent in soups and gumbos. I suppose you are wondering if it is a vegetable you could serve to your best friends. Well, when we serve it as a vegetable at Miss Ruby's, guests who aren't from the South would ask, "What is that?" We simply say, "Try it. If you don't like it, we'll serve you something else." Most times, they ask for an extra order.

2 pounds fresh okra (frozen may be used)
4 tablespoons peanut oil (we recommend Louana)
½ pound thick-sliced bacon, chopped
1½ cups white onions, finely chopped
1 cup green onions, thinly sliced
6 medium cloves fresh garlic, minced
1½ cups fresh tomatoes, diced (peel and all)
½ cup parsley, very finely chopped
1½ teaspoons garlic powder
1 teaspoon garlic salt
1 teaspoon white pepper
1 teaspoon black pepper
½ teaspoon cayenne pepper
1 teaspoon creole seasoning (we recommend Tony's)
½ teaspoon Lawry's seasoned salt
1 can (16 ounces) whole tomatoes

Wash, stem, and cut the okra into ½-inch pieces. Place the peanut oil in a heavy skillet (cast iron preferred) over medium heat and allow it to become hot before adding the okra. Sauté for 10 minutes or until the okra is no longer stringy; drain in a colander and set aside. Meanwhile, place the chopped bacon in a heavy saucepan and cook until it is crisp. Add the white onion, green onion, fresh garlic, fresh tomatoes, and parsley, and sauté for 15 minutes. Add the seasonings, okra, and canned tomatoes (squeeze each one by hand) with their juice. Reduce heat and cook for about 30 minutes. Stir occasionally to prevent sticking and to blend the seasonings. It is now ready to serve but keeps well and may be reheated.

SERVES 8.

Leftovers may be frozen or kept in the refrigerator for several days. Serve with pork chops, fried chicken, country fried steak, ham — almost anything.

❧ Oven-Browned Potatoes

4 large Idaho or baking potatoes
½ teaspoon salt
½ teaspoon white pepper
½ teaspoon black pepper
½ teaspoon Lawry's seasoned salt
1½ teaspoons paprika (for color)
Dash garlic powder
¼ cup butter or margarine, melted

Peel the potatoes and cut them into 1-inch cubes. Place the cubed potatoes in a baking pan and season. Pour melted butter or margarine over the seasoned potato cubes and stir to coat all sides. Place in a 350-degree oven and cook until tender and slightly browned. Turn the potatoes several times while baking to ensure all sides are cooked evenly.

SERVES 6.

❧ Grandmother Carr's Spanish Corn

1 pound sliced bacon
1 large white onion (about 3 inches in diameter), finely chopped
12 ears fresh yellow corn, cut off of the cobs (scrape the corn for the milk)
1 can (15 ounces) tomato sauce
1 teaspoon sugar

In a heavy Dutch oven (preferably iron), fry the bacon until it is crisp. Drain well on paper towels and set aside for garnish. Retain half of the bacon drippings in the Dutch oven. Cool slightly before adding the chopped onion, cut corn, and tomato sauce. Bring to a boil and then lower the heat. Simmer until the corn is done and add the sugar to cut the tartness. If any grease rises to the surface, be sure to skim it off. Pour into a casserole dish and top with crumbled bacon. Be sure to serve piping hot.

SERVES 8 TO 10.

One of my dear friends and great customers, Dick Carr, always talked about his grandmother's wonderful corn dish and what a great cook she was. Dick manages an antique shop on Royal Street and ate with us at Miss Ruby's almost every night for two years.

We had to do a lot of searching to come up with this recipe. I know you will enjoy it as much as I have. I want to dedicate this to Florance Stewart Carr of Pensacola, Florida. We were finally able to get the recipe from Dick's Aunt while having dinner with her at the Biltmore Hotel in Miami, Christmas 1989.

❦ Rod's Grilled Onions

6 medium onions
6 beef bouillon cubes
6 pats butter or margarine
Cayenne pepper, to taste

With a sharp paring knife, cut off the root-end each onion so that it sits flat. Peel the onions and hollow out the top center of each (about ½ inch wide and ½ inch deep). Set each onion in the middle of a 6-inch square of foil. Put one whole bouillon cube in each onion and top with a pat of butter. Sprinkle lightly with cayenne pepper. Close the foil by twisting and squeezing the four corners together to make a point on top or a "handle." Place on a hot grill for 30 minutes or bake in a 350-degree oven. To serve, remove the foil and place on the plate with steak or any other meat.

SERVES 6.

My son, Rod, has cooked these for me, high in the mountains of Washington state and in my French Quarter garden. They are easy to prepare and very good, too.

❦ B's Lima Beans

2 pounds large dried lima beans
3 bay leaves
½ stick butter or margaine
1 large onion, chopped
5 cloves garlic, minced
1 pound smoked beef sausage, sliced
1 teaspoon thyme
¼ teaspoon cayenne pepper
Salt and freshly ground black pepper, to taste
½ red bell pepper, cut in slivers for color

Wash the beans well and put them in a pot; cover with water and soak overnight. Do not wash the beans again or you will lose some of the vitamins. The next day, place the beans and bay leaves in a large pot with plenty of water (about 3 inches above the beans). Cook over medium heat until beans start to get tender. Meanwhile, melt the butter or margarine in a large skillet and sauté the onion, garlic, and sausage over medium heat. Add this to the beans when they are tender and continue cooking. Add the seasonings and more water as needed. Be sure to stir often as the "soup" thickens or the beans will stick and scorch quickly. Add the red bell pepper at the end for color.

SERVES 10 TO 12.

This recipe was given to me by my dear French Quarter friend, B. Smith, who is well-known for her primitive paintings and portraits. She is also a fantastic cook. Her father was a doctor in Bay St. Louis, Mississippi. When she paints and cooks, she recalls the way things were done in her home when she was a child.

❦ Stuffed Broiled Tomatoes

4 tomatoes
2 tablespoons olive oil
¼ cup celery, chopped
¼ cup green bell pepper, finely chopped
1 large clove garlic, minced
1 tablespoon fresh parsley, chopped
8 medium shrimp, peeled and deveined
½ pound lump crabmeat
4 tablespoons dried bread crumbs
Salt and freshly ground black pepper, to taste
1 tablespoon Parmesan or Romano cheese, grated

Preheat the oven to 350 degrees. Cut a slice from the stem end of each unpeeled tomato and scoop out the center pulp. Dice the tomato pulp and set aside. Heat the olive oil in a heavy skillet or saucepan and add the celery, bell pepper, garlic, parsley, tomato pulp, and shrimp, and cook for 2 to 3 minutes over medium heat. Then, add the crabmeat, bread crumbs, salt, and pepper. Stir gently so the lumps of crabmeat will not break apart. Stuff each scooped-out tomato with this mixture and arrange in a shallow baking dish. Sprinkle the Parmesan or Romano cheese over the top and bake for 25 to 30 minutes.

As an alternative, substitute ½ cup fully cooked, chopped ham and 4 slices cooked, crumbled bacon for the shrimp and crab.

SERVES 4.

This dish can be prepared in advance and kept covered in the refrigerator until time to bake and serve. It makes an excellent side dish with any meat or fowl that go well with tomatoes. It's especially beautiful when served beside Braised Celery (see page 157) with duck. It's also wonderful as a light main course, served with fresh green beans and a green salad. B. Smith, an artist friend of mine, shared this recipe with me — it's a favorite.

❦ Chef Mason's Creamy Red Beans

2 pounds red beans
4 bay leaves
1 ham bone with meat
1 pound pickled pork, cut into 2-inch cubes
¼ cup peanut oil
2 large onions, chopped
7 stalks celery, chopped
1 teaspoon garlic
1 tablespoon sugar
½ teaspoon Ac'cent flavor enhancer (optional)
¼ cup fresh parsley, finely chopped
Salt and pepper, to taste (*do not* add salt until the very end because the
    ham and pickled meat usually add all the salt that is necessary)

Most red bean recipes call for the beans to be soaked overnight. Chef
Mason, whose award-winning red beans are some of the best in New
Orleans, does not soak his beans. Instead, he cooks the beans for an hour
and a half before adding most of the ingredients. This softens the beans up,
just like soaking them overnight does. Chef Mason says that the water the
unsoaked beans cook in has all sorts of nutrients; this is one of the secrets of
great red beans. If you really want to soak the beans, be sure *not* to pour off
the water in which they soaked. *Do not* rinse the beans.

Put the beans into a very large pot and cover with water. The proportion
is one part beans to two parts water. Add the bay leaves and ham bone (cut
any meat off the bone, chop into 2-inch cubes, and set aside). Bring to a boil,
reduce to medium heat, and cover. Cook at a fast simmer for 1½ hours.

Meanwhile, sauté the ham, pickled pork, onion, celery, and garlic over
medium heat. Set aside.

After the beans cook for 1½ hours, add the sautéed seasonings, sugar,
Ac'cent, parsley, and pepper. Cover and continue to simmer slowly for at
least another 1½ hours. Stir occasionally. Before serving, taste for salt, and
add as necessary.

The longer the beans cook, the creamier they get and the better they taste.
To make the beans creamy faster, uncover the pot and cook over a slightly
higher heat.

For a great meal, serve the beans over a mound of rice with sausage or
ham on the side.

❦ Braised Celery

4 small bunches celery hearts
2 slices bacon, cut in pieces
2 tablespoons shallots, finely chopped
1 large carrot, finely chopped
1 tablespoon fresh parsley, finely chopped
1 bay leaf
1 cup chicken broth
3 tablespoons lemon juice
Salt and freshly ground pepper, to taste
2 teaspoons butter or margarine
4 teaspoons flour

Preheat the oven to 350 degrees. Wash the celery hearts, remove any blemishes, cut down to 4 inches, and slice in half (use only the end of the bunch). Tie the stalks together with kitchen string and arrange them on the bottom of a buttered casserole dish. Fry the bacon until crisp. Add the shallots, carrot, parsley, and bay leaf, and sauté for another 3 minutes. Then, stir in the chicken broth, lemon juice, salt, and pepper. Bring to a boil, reduce the heat, and simmer for 5 minutes more. Pour over the celery. Cover the dish with foil and place in the preheated oven for 40 minutes or until tender.

At serving time, remove the celery from the casserole, take off the string, and arrange on a preheated platter. Set aside and keep warm. Put the casserole on top of the stove, mix the butter and flour together, and add to the liquid. Bring the liquid to a boil and then strain. Pour over the celery and garnish with chopped fresh parsley.

SERVES 4.

This is an excellent side dish with many entrées.

❦ Baked Beans

4 slices bacon
½ cup chopped onion
2 cans (16 ounces each) pork and beans with tomato sauce
2 tablespoons brown sugar
1 tablespoon Worcestershire sauce (we recommend Lea & Perrin's)
1 teaspoon prepared mustard
¼ cup catsup

Fry the bacon in a large skillet until crisp and reserve the drippings.
Drain the bacon well on a paper towel and crumble when cool. In the reserved drippings, cook the chopped onion until tender but not brown. Add pork and beans, brown sugar, Worcestershire sauce, mustard, catsup, and crumbled bacon to the onion in the skillet and mix well. Turn the mixture into a 1½-quart casserole and bake uncovered in a 350-degree oven for about 1 hour.

SERVES 8.

Baked Beans are excellent served with barbecue.

❦ Ratatouille

1 medium eggplant
6 medium tomatoes
3 medium zucchini squash
3 medium bell peppers
¼ cup peanut oil
¼ cup olive oil
3 medium cloves garlic, minced
3 tablespoons green onions, finely chopped
Salt and freshly ground black pepper, to taste
1 tablespoon fresh parsley, chopped

Remove the stem from the eggplant. Cut the eggplant into four parts lengthwise and then slice crosswise at ½-inch intervals. Peel the tomatoes and cut into small wedges. Slice the zucchini in ½-inch pieces. Seed the bell peppers and cut them in thin strips about 1 inch long. When the vegetables are prepared, heat the peanut oil and olive oil in a heavy skillet, and sauté the garlic and green onion until tender. Add all the vegetables and brown slightly. Season with salt and pepper, and add the parsley. Cover the skillet and simmer over a low flame until the vegetables are done. Be sure to stir occasionally. Serve in a small preheated vegetable dish.

SERVES 8.

Ratatouille is great served cold as an appetizer.

❦ *Vegetable Pasta*

½ cup butter or olive oil
1 large onion, coarsely chopped
1 cup green onions, chopped
½ cup celery, thinly sliced
2 fresh tomatoes, cut in small wedges
1 teaspoon onion powder
1 teaspoon garlic powder
1 teaspoon white pepper
1 teaspoon freshly ground black pepper
½ teaspoon garlic salt
½ teaspoon Tony Cacherie's creole seasoning
½ teaspoon chicken base or salt
1 pound egg noodles

Sauté all of the above ingredients together in a large skillet or sauté pan. Leave the vegetables crisp.
   Serve over a bed of egg noodles.

SERVES 4 TO 6.

Vegetable Pasta is excellent with veal or any meat.

❦ Eggplant Soufflé

1 medium eggplant
2 tablespoons butter
2 tablespoons flour
1 cup milk
½ cup Parmesan cheese, freshly grated
¾ cup soft bread crumbs
¼ cup onion, minced
Salt and freshly ground black pepper, to taste
¼ teaspoon thyme, finely ground
2 eggs, separated

Peel the eggplant. Cut in pieces and cook in a pot of salted water until tender. Drain the eggplant well and mash very fine. Melt the butter in a saucepan, and add the flour; when smooth and blended, add the milk and stir until thickened. Add the eggplant, Parmesan cheese, bread crumbs, onion, salt, pepper, thyme and egg yolks which should be beaten until they are light. Whip the egg whites until they are stiff and fold them gently into the mixture. Turn into a greased baking dish; set in hot water and bake in a moderate oven (325 degrees) until the test knife come out clean (approximately 30 to 45 minutes).

SERVES 6.

❦ Refried Beans

1 pound pinto beans
1 bell pepper, chopped
2 large onions, chopped
5 cloves garlic, minced
¼ cup olive oil
½ cup cheddar cheese, shredded
1 pound fresh sausage (Chaurice is best)
Salt and pepper, to taste

Soak the pinto beans in water overnight. The next day, drain and rinse the beans well. Place the beans in a large pot and cover them with water. Be sure the water level is about 2 inches above the beans. Add the chopped bell pepper, one of the large chopped onions, 3 cloves of the minced garlic, and salt to the pot, and cook over medium heat until the beans are tender.

In a separate pan, sauté the remaining chopped onion and garlic in the olive oil until tender.

In a heavy iron skillet, fry the sausage and crumble it after cooking. Add the beans and the garlic and onion mixture to the skillet with the crumbled sausage and cook together over a low heat for 10 minutes. Mash the mixture with a potato masher. Just before serving, sprinkle generously with shredded cheese and run under the broiler to melt.

SERVES 12.

❦ *Potatoes au Gratin*

4 Idaho potatoes
Salt and freshly ground pepper, to taste
½ cup butter or margarine
½ cup grated Parmesan cheese
½ cup grated American cheese
¼ cup heavy cream

Preheat the oven to 375 degrees. Peel, wash, dry, and cut the potatoes into thin slices. Butter a flameproof casserole or baking dish and place a layer of the sliced potatoes on the bottom of the dish. Melt the butter in a saucepan and pour some of it over the layer of potatoes. Sprinkle with salt, pepper, and cheeses. Continue adding potatoes, butter, salt, pepper, and cheeses in layers until all the ingredients are used. Pour the heavy cream over the mixture and cover with aluminum foil. Place the dish into the preheated oven and bake for 1 hour. About 10 minutes before serving, remove the foil to allow the potatoes to turn a golden-brown.

SERVES 8 TO 10.

❦ Carolyn's Hearts of Artichoke and Mushroom Casserole

2 cans (16 ounces each) artichoke hearts
1 pound fresh mushrooms
1 bottle (12 ounces) olive oil
3 cloves garlic, minced
½ cup Parmesan cheese
1 medium can Italian bread crumbs
Salt and freshly ground black pepper, to taste

Drain the artichoke hearts and wash the mushrooms. Save the water for use later on. Slice the mushrooms and put them in a skillet with the olive oil. Cook for a short time before adding the artichoke hearts which should be halved or quartered. Add the fresh garlic and fry briefly. Add half of the cheese and simmer a short time. Add the water that was saved and stir lightly so the artichoke hearts will not break up. Add the bread crumbs and the balance of the cheese, reserving some to sprinkle on top of the casserole. If the mixture is not mushy enough, add more tap water. Place in a baking dish and top with Parmesan cheese. Just before serving, bake in a 350-degree oven for approximately 15 minutes or until bubbly and slightly browned.

SERVES 8.

This recipe is good made into balls for hor d'oeuvres but the artichoke hearts and mushrooms must be chopped very finely.

❦ White Cabbage with Butter

1 large head white cabbage
1 stick butter
¼ cup water
Salt and freshly ground black pepper, to taste

Preheat the oven to 350 degrees. Remove the outer leaves from the cabbage and quarter it. Remove the center core and then cut the cabbage into 1-inch wedges.

Butter a deep casserole or baking dish and pour in the water. Place a layer of shredded cabbage in the bottom of the dish, sprinkle with salt and pepper, and dot the layer with small pieces of butter. Repeat the layers until all of the cabbage is used. Be sure to save a little of the butter for the top. Cover tightly with aluminum foil and bake for approximately 30 minutes. Serve immediately.

SERVES 6 TO 8.

This dish is guaranteed to make everyone a cabbage fan.

❦ Candied Yams

4 large sweet potatoes
2 cups sugar
½ cup water
1 stick butter or margarine
1 teaspoon lemon juice
1 teaspoon cinnamon

Boil the sweet potatoes whole until they are fork-tender and remove them from the water to cool. Place the sugar and water in a saucepan and boil over medium heat for 30 minutes to make a syrup. Then, add the butter or margarine and lemon juice to the syrup.

Meanwhile, peel and slice the sweet potatoes into ½-inch slices and place them in a baking dish. Sprinkle the cinnamon over the potatoes and add the syrup. Bake for 30 minutes at 350 degrees.

This is an unusual way to prepare candied yams, but it is the best. This recipe was given to me by my good friend, the late Germaine C. Wells, and her life-long personal cook, Lucinda.

❦ Eggplant Stuffed with Shrimp and Crab

6 large eggplants
1 cup butter
1½ cups onions, chopped
1½ cups celery, chopped
2 cups green onions, chopped
7 cloves garlic, minced
1 cup bell pepper, chopped
1 cup parsley, chopped
½ teaspoon poultry seasoning
1 teaspoon black pepper
½ teaspoon Italian seasoning
½ teaspoon sage
½ teaspoon oregano
1 teaspoon garlic salt
2 teaspoons Lawry's seasoned salt
1 teaspoon cayenne pepper
2½ teaspoons garlic powder
2½ teaspoons onion powder
1½ teaspoons chicken base or chicken bouillon cubes by Knorr
2 cups medium shrimp, peeled and deveined
1 cup special white crabmeat
2½ cups unseasoned bread crumbs
1½ sticks butter or margarine

Place the eggplant in a large pot and cover with water (use two pots if necessary). Boil over medium heat for 30 minutes or until the eggplant is tender. Drain and set aside to cool — do not peel.

Melt the butter in a large heavy skillet and add the onion, celery, green onion, garlic, bell pepper, and parsley, and sauté until tender. Add all the seasonings and cook for 10 minutes. Once the eggplants are cooled, split each one lengthwise, and scoop out and mash the flesh. Save the shells to stuff with the seafood dressing. Now, add the mashed eggplant to the seasoned vegetables and cook for 10 more minutes over low heat, stirring frequently. Then, add the shrimp and cook slowly for 15 minutes. Add the crabmeat and 1½ cups of bread crumbs, and mix well. Fill the eggplant

— Sock it to me Cake —

filling
2 tb cake mix
2 tp cinnamon
2 tlb brown sugar
1 cup pecans chopped

Cake mix w/ Sour cream
1/2 C Crisco oil
1/4 C sugar
1/4 C water
4 eggs

beat for 2 min
pour 2/3 of batter into
pan — pour filling —
pour the rest on top
@ 350 for 45 to 55 min

shells with the seafood dressing and place in individual oven-proof casserole dishes or side-by-side in long Pyrex baking dish. They may be covered and refrigerated until ready to serve or individually wrapped and frozen.

When ready to serve, sprinkle with bread crumbs, garnish with one or two peeled, deveined raw shrimp, and drizzle butter over the top. Bake in a 350-degree oven for 15 to 20 minutes or until it bubbles. Run under the broiler to brown slightly.

I know you are saying that this is a complicated dish but, if you ever order Stuffed Eggplant at Miss Ruby's, this is the exact recipe we use. It is spicy and delicious.

❦ *Louisiana Creole Red Beans*

1 pound red beans
1½ cups onion, finely chopped
1 cup green onions, chopped
3 cloves garlic, minced
1 cup bell pepper, chopped
4 bay leaves
1 teaspoon creole seasoning (we recommend Tony's)
¼ teaspoon cayenne pepper
6 ham hocks or 1 cup chopped ham
10 cups water

Wash the beans well and soak in water overnight. Drain and remove any discolored beans. In a 4-quart pan, sauté the onion, green onion, garlic, bell pepper, bay leaves, creole seasoning, and cayenne pepper in oil for 5 to 10 minutes or until onions are done. Add the beans to the pot, along with the ham; cover with enough cold water to be approximately 2 inches over the contents. Bring to a rapid boil; reduce heat and cook slowly for 2 to 3 hours or until the beans are tender and creamy.

Serve over a mound of rice with smoked creole sausage.

SERVES 8.

Eggs, Rice and Pasta

❦ Rod's Gourmet Omelet

2 large eggs, well-beaten
2 tablespoons water
2 tablespoons clarified butter
1 kiwi fruit, peeled and thinly sliced
½ banana, peeled and thinly sliced
4 strawberries, thinly sliced
2 tablespoons powdered sugar
2 tablespoons sour cream
1 ounce apricot brandy

Assemble and prepare all the ingredients. Whip the eggs and water in a blender or with a wire whisk until they are fluffy. Place the clarified butter in an omelet pan and heat. Pour in the egg mixture and when the omelet sets, place the fruit on the left half of the eggs — first the kiwi fruit in a straight row, then the bananas in another row, and finally the strawberries. Sprinkle the powdered sugar over the fruit and fold the omelet from right to left. Place the omelet on a flameproof platter and pour the brandy over it. Ignite with a long match and allow it to flame while carrying it to the table. When the flame goes out, baste the omelet with the brandy remaining in the dish. Top with sour cream and cut into 2 to 4 pieces. This is a pretty and exciting way to serve a light dessert with very little work.

SERVES 2 TO 4.

This recipe was given to me by my son, Rod Smart, who lives in Washington state. You can use the basic omelet recipe for many variation. Try onions, ham and cheese, crab and shrimp, or anything you may have in your refrigerator that you wish to use. The variations are limitless, so use your imagination and enjoy.

❦ Omelet Supreme
from Miss Ruby's Other Place

3 large eggs
3 tablespoons butter or margarine
¼ cup ham, chopped in cubes
2 slices bacon, cooked crisp and crumbled
1 slice onion, chopped
2 slices mild cheddar cheese
4 mushrooms, sliced
¼ cup hash brown potatoes or french fries, cubed
½ small bell pepper, chopped

Melt the butter or margarine in a large omelet pan, add all the vegetables and meat, and cook, using a spatula to lift and turn the vegetables, until tender. Place the eggs in a blender and whip them long enough to make them fluffy. Pour at once over the vegetables and meat, and place the cheese on top. When the eggs are set, fold the omelet over. This is enough for a full course meal at any time of day. It is so large it must be served on a platter.

Miss Ruby's Other Place was a beautiful small restaurant located at 839 Bienville in the French Quarter. We served breakfast there until 2 o'clock in the afternoon. This dish was a very popular lunch item we served with a small house salad. The recipe came from one of my young chefs.

❦ Eggs Benedict

4 English muffins, split
8 thin slices Canadian bacon
8 poached eggs
½ cup warm Hollandaise Sauce (see page 187)

Place the muffins, split side up, in a preheated oven and toast. Remove and keep warm. Cook the Canadian bacon slices. Meanwhile, poach the eggs. Arrange 2 muffin halves, toasted side up, on a warm serving plate. Put a slice of Canadian bacon on each half and top with a poached egg. Spoon warm Hollandaise Sauce over the eggs and garnish with ripe olives, capers, parsley, black caviar, or paprika.

SERVES 4.

❦ Rice Pilaf

½ cup butter or margarine
2 cups long grain white rice
3 cups well-flavored chicken broth, free of fat

Melt the butter in a heavy flameproof casserole and add the rice. Cook over low heat for 1 minute, then pour in the chicken broth. Bring to a boil, reduce heat, and cover. Simmer 12 to 15 minutes or until all the liquid is absorbed. Do not stir. Serve immediately.

❦ Lupita's Fried Rice

3 tablespoons peanut oil
1 large onion, minced
2 cloves garlic, minced
Salt and freshly ground black pepper, to taste
1 large tomato, chopped
2 cups long grain white rice, uncooked
3 cups chicken stock
½ package frozen peas and carrots

Sauté the onion, garlic, salt, and pepper in the peanut oil over low heat until tender. Add the tomato and cook lightly before adding the rice. Stir well and add the chicken stock, peas, and carrots. Then, cover the pot and cook over a low heat for 15 to 20 minutes.

SERVES 6 TO 8.

❦ Moran's Fettuccine

3 quarts water
½ teaspoon salt
1 pound green or white fresh fettuccine noodles
¼ pound butter or margarine at room temperature
⅓ pound Parmesan cheese, grated
¼ cup half-and-half, at room temperature, or broth from fettuccine
Salt and freshly ground black pepper, to taste

Bring the salted water to a vigorous boil and drop in the fettuccine, stirring until all the noodles are separated. Boil for approximately 1 minute for white fettuccine and 3 minutes for green fettuccine (overcooking will ruin the noodles), and drain loosely, leaving a little water on the noodles. Add the butter and mix well with a fork and spoon. Add the cheese and mix well to avoid lumping. Add the cream or broth and mix thoroughly until the mixture is loose and creamy.

Jimmy Moran says successful fettuccine is determined by the consistency. It should be neither be watery nor dry. Add a little liquid if necessary until the proper smooth, creamy consistency is reached. Serve immediately, topped with freshly ground black pepper.

SERVES 4.

We purchase our fresh pasta from Moran's Pastificio on the ground level of Moran's Riverside Restaurant, located at 44 French Market Place where Dumaine Street meets the Mississippi River in New Orleans.

❦ *Creamy Macaroni and Cheese*

1½ cups elbow macaroni
3 tablespoons margarine
3 tablespoons flour
½ teaspoon salt, or to taste
2 cups milk
8 ounces American cheese slices
1 cup bread crumbs

Cook the macaroni in salted, boiling water until tender, and drain. In a saucepan, melt the butter and blend in the flour and salt. Add 2 cups of milk and cook until thick and bubbly. Add the American cheese and stir until melted. Mix the cheese sauce and the macaroni together and place in a 1½-quart casserole. Sprinkle the bread crumbs over the top and bake at 350 degrees for 30 minutes, or until bubbly and light brown.

SERVES 8 TO 10.

At Miss Ruby's, we serve this with meat loaf, turnip greens, and cornbread muffins.

This dish is so popular people ask for side orders. When it isn't on the menu, customers are disappointed.

Stocks and Sauces

❧ Chef Mason's Basic Italian Tomato Sauce or Tomato Gravy

3 large onions, finely chopped
7 stalks celery, finely chopped
½ cup olive oil
1 tablespoon garlic, minced
2 cans (6 ounces each) tomato paste
4 cans (16 ounces each) whole tomatoes, crushed
3 cans (15 ounces each) tomato sauce
2 cups water
4 bay leaves
1 tablespoon oregano, preferably fresh
1 tablespoon basil, preferably fresh
1 tablespoon Italian seasoning
½ cup grated Parmesan cheese
2 generous dashes Worcestershire sauce
Salt and pepper, to taste
1½ tablespoons sugar
¼ cup fresh parsley, finely chopped
2 pig's feet (optional)

Chop the onion and celery by hand, or use a food processor. In a large pot, sauté the onions and celery in olive oil over medium heat for 10 minutes, or until tender. Add the garlic and tomato paste and continue to cook over low heat. Add the crushed tomatoes, tomato sauce, water, seasonings, Parmesan cheese, and sugar. Add the fresh parsley and pig's feet and cook slowly for at least 2 hours.

> *Chef Mason says that the longer the sauce cooks, the better it gets. Using pig's feet to season the sauce comes from an old creole recipe for Italian tomato gravy and, according to Chef Mason, that's what makes this recipe so tasty and so special.*

🦞 Garlic Mayonnaise

8 large cloves garlic
½ teaspoon salt
1 tablespoon white wine vinegar or to taste
2 egg yolks
1½ cups olive oil
1 tablepoon lemon juice
Freshly ground black pepper, to taste

Halve the garlic cloves, remove the green fibers from the middle if there are any, and chop them coarsely. Pile them in a mortar and pestle, and pound them with the salt until they form a smooth paste, or crush them with the salt using the back of a chef's knife.

Transfer the garlic to a mixing bowl or food processor and add the vinegar and egg yolks. Beat well until the yolks start to thicken and then add the olive oil a few drops at a time. When the mayonnaise begins to thicken, add the oil in a thin steady stream.

WATCHPOINT: If the mayonnaise curdles and separates, it can be brought back and corrected by placing a fresh egg yolk in a clean bowl and gradually adding the mayonnaise to it.

When the oil is all incorporated, beat in the lemon juice and black pepper, and taste for seasoning. If the texture is thicker than you like, thin with a 1 to 2 tablespoons of warm water.

Put the mayonnaise in a bowl and serve it with raw or cooked vegetables, fried crab claws, fried oysters, or hot, crusty French bread. Also excellent on our Fried Oyster Loaf (see page 134).

❦ Miss Ruby's French Dressing

1 cup olive oil
⅓ cup red wine vinegar
¼ teaspoon freshly ground black pepper
¼ teaspoon salt
1 clove garlic, minced
1 teaspoon fresh mint, minced (optional)
¼ teaspoon oregano

Place all the ingredients in a bottle and allow to stand for a few minutes or longer. Shake vigorously and serve.

❦ Giblet Gravy

2 tablespoons margarine
4 tablespoons flour
½ teaspoon salt (use less salt if you use the broth from the turkey)
¼ teaspoon black pepper
3 cups chicken stock
1 cup broth form the turkey pan
¼ pound chicken livers, boiled and finely chopped (use gizzards, heart, livers and neck of turkey if available instead of chicken livers)
3 hard-boiled eggs, finely chopped

While the turkey is cooking, slowly boil the giblets until they are tender.
In a saucepan, melt the margarine over medium heat. Gradually add the flour, salt, and pepper, and brown slightly. Then, add the chicken broth and broth from the turkey pan and cook until creamy. Add the liver, other chopped giblets, and the eggs. Cook until the gravy is slightly thickened, and then cook another 5 minutes.
Serve over chicken or turkey with bread dressing and cranberry sauce on the side.

SERVES 8 TO 10.

❦ Miss Jean's Tartar Sauce

1 medium onion
¼ cup sweet pickle relish
1 pint mayonnaise
Dash cayenne pepper (optional)

Peel and quarter the onion. Place it in a food processor and chop finely.
Add the pickle relish and mayonnaise, and mix on low speed for 1 minute.
If you like it a little spicy, add the cayenne pepper.

*This will keep in the refrigerator for 2 to 3 weeks. It's so easy to make but
it's the best!*

❦ Chef Oscar's Bar-B-Que Sauce

5 cups catsup
¼ cup Worcestershire sauce
9 cloves garlic
½ cup yellow mustard
1 cup light brown sugar
3 tablespoons liquid smoke
2 teaspoons black pepper
2 teaspoons garlic powder
2 teaspoons onion powder
¼ cup fresh lemon juice
2 teaspoons white pepper
½ teaspoon cayenne pepper

This sauce does not have to be cooked. Simply beat ingredients together
well with a wire whisk. This sauce may be refrigerated in a covered
container for 30 days or more.

MAKES 2 QUARTS.

*We use this sauce on ribs, chicken, barbecued beef, and anything else
requiring a barbecue sauce.*

❧ Basic Roux

The phrase, "First you make a roux," is repeated in countless creole and Cajun recipes. A roux is a mixture of oil (cooking oil, butter, or bacon grease) and flour, cooked in a heavy pot or skillet over low heat, until the flour turns an even nut-brown or darker. Some recipes call for a light, cream-colored roux which simply indicates less cooking time. The process takes approximately 20 to 25 minutes and requires constant stirring because, if the flour burns, it will not thicken properly and will impart an unpleasant taste.

Roux may be made ahead of time and, if stored in a tightly covered container, will keep in the refrigerator or the freezer for a long time.

Proportion: ¾ cup oil to 1 cup flour (enough flour to absorb the oil and to make a smooth paste).

All the creole and Cajun gumbos call for a roux.

❧ Lupita's Basque Salsa

9 fresh tomatoes (may substitute 1½ 16-ounce cans stewed tomatoes, but
    fresh is best)
7 jalapeño peppers
4 cloves fresh garlic
1 tablespoon salt, or to taste
½ teaspoon oregano
1 bunch green onions, chopped
2 large avocados, cut into small wedges

Cook tomatoes and jalapeños together until tender. Set aside to cool.

Using a mortar and pestle, crush the garlic and salt together. Add the jalapeños and crush again. Put this mixture into a bowl. Peel the skin off the tomatoes. Mash the tomatoes with the mortar and pestle. Put the crushed tomatoes into the bowl with the other ingredients. Mix well. Sprinkle with oregano, add green onions and avocado, and mix lightly.

Serve with anything that requires salsa.

This salsa is best if the peppers and tomatoes are left chunky.

❦ Creole Sauce

1 cup margarine
1 cup onion, chopped julienne-style
1 cup celery, chopped julienne-style
1 cup bell pepper, chopped julienne-style
1 cup green onions, chopped
4 cloves garlic, minced
1½ cups fresh tomatoes, cut into chunks
6 cups chicken stock
2 teaspoons onion powder
2 teaspoons garlic powder
1 teaspoon garlic salt
½ teaspoon Lawry's seasoned salt
1 teaspoon black pepper
1 teaspoon salt or chicken base or chicken-flavored bouillon cubes by
   Knorr
½ teaspoon white pepper
Dash of cayenne pepper
1 can (6 ounces) tomato paste
2 cups tomato purée
2 teaspoons sugar

In a large pot, melt the margarine. Add the onion, celery, bell pepper, green onion, garlic, and tomatoes. Cook slowly for 10 minutes, stirring frequently. Then, add the remaining ingredients. Cook slowly for 45 minutes, stirring occasionally to prevent sticking.

MAKES APPROXIMATELY 1 GALLON.

This sauce can be used for the following entrées:
   Redfish Courtbouillon
   Creole Chicken
   Creole Meatloaf
   Creole Pork Chops
   Shrimp Creole

❦ Red Cocktail Sauce

1 cup catsup
1 tablespoon horseradish
1 tablespoon Louisiana hot sauce or Tabasco sauce
Juice of ½ lemon

Mix ingredients together well. Will keep in the refrigerator for 30 days or more.

SERVES 6.

❦ Bechemel or White Wine Sauce

1 cup butter or margarine, melted
½ cup flour
1 teaspoon onion powder
1 teaspoon garlic powder
2 teaspoons salt or chicken base or chicken-flavored bouillon cubes by
  Knorr
2 cups milk
1 teaspoon white pepper
3 cups chicken stock
1 ounce white wine

Over a slow heat, add flour to melted margarine, stirring until smooth. Add onion powder, garlic powder, and salt or chicken base, mixing well. Add milk, stirring constantly until thickened. Add white pepper and chicken stock, and continue to cook slowly for 35 minutes, stirring constantly. Add white wine, and stir well. Sauce will be creamy and smooth.

Will keep in the refrigerator 7 days or, frozen in small containers, up to 3 months.

MAKES APPROXIMATELY 1 GALLON.

This recipe may be used in any recipe calling for a white wine sauce.

❧ Bouquet Garni

2 sprigs parsley
1 bay leaf
1 stalk celery, including tops

Tie the parsley, bay leaf, and celery in a cheesecloth with kitchen string. Bouquet Garni is added to many recipes to add the flavor of parsley, celery, and bay leaves. It is removed before serving. You may include any other ingredients you wish to use for flavor only.

❧ Basic White Sauce

1 cup butter or margarine, melted
½ cup flour
1 teaspoon onion powder
1 teaspoon garlic powder
2 teaspoons salt or chicken base or chicken-flavored bouillon cubes by
    Knorr
2 cups milk
1 teaspoon white pepper
3 cups chicken stock

Over a slow heat, add flour to melted butter, stirring until smooth. Add onion powder, garlic powder, and salt or chicken base, mixing well. Add milk, stirring constantly until thickened. Add white pepper and chicken stock, and continue to cook slowly for 35 minutes, stirring constantly. Sauce will be creamy and smooth.
    Will keep in refrigerator for 7 days.

MAKES APPROXIMATELY 1 GALLON.

This sauce can be used on veal, chicken, potatoes au gratin, or with any recipe calling for a white sauce.

❦ Brown Butter Sauce

1 pound butter
2 cups chopped green onions
9 cloves garlic
1 teaspoon onion powder
1 teaspoon white pepper
1 teaspoon black pepper
2 teaspoons garlic powder
1 teaspoon season salt
1 teaspoon beef base (or beef bouillon granules) or salt
1 cup flour
1 gallon beef stock
1½ tablespoons Wright's Kitchen Bouquet

Sauté the green onions and garlic in the butter. Add all the spices. Slowly add the flour, stirring until smooth. Add the beef stock and Kitchen Bouquet, and cook slowly for 1½ hours, stirring occasionally to prevent sticking.

After cooking, this sauce must be strained. If it is used immediately, it will keep in the refrigerator for about 7 days.

This recipe may be adjusted for smaller quantities.

MAKES 1 GALLON.

Can be used on Sautéed Redfish, Chicken Cordon Bleu, or with any recipe calling for a brown sauce.

❦ Miss Ruby's Remoulade Sauce

2 jars (16 ounces each) Zatarain's Creole Mustard
Scant ¾ cup white vinegar
2 cups extra virgin olive oil
1 tablespoon salt, or less, depending on taste.
2 tablespoons white pepper
1 cup parsley, very finely chopped
2 large onions, very finely chopped (use food processor if possible)
1 cup green onions, very finely chopped by hand
2 hearts of celery, very finely chopped (use food processor or blender if possible)
1 can (1 ounce) paprika, for color

Place all ingredients in a large bowl. Mix with a whisk until well-blended. Pour into a jar, cover, and refrigerate. Will keep for about 2 weeks.

MAKES ABOUT ½ GALLON.

This is the original recipe from a very famous New Orleans restaurant owned by my dear friend, the late Germaine Wells. Germaine was known all over the world for this wonderful remoulade sauce, which was created for her by Chef Josef. The recipe came to me through Chef Josef's daughter-in-law, Catherine Barras.

❦ Basic Beef Stock

2 pounds bone and scraps of beef
6 stalks celery, cut up
2 medium onions, quartered
1 head garlic, peeled

Boil all ingredients slowly for 2 hours. Use no salt in the stock. Strain the stock, and refrigerate or freeze.

❦ Basic Chicken Stock

3 pounds chicken parts (no livers)
3 gallons water
6 stalks celery, cut up
3 medium onions, quartered

Boil the chicken slowly in the water for 2 hours. Strain the stock through a colander. Use no salt in the stock. Refrigerate or freeze if you're not using the stock immediately.

❦ Basic Hollandaise Sauce

3 egg yolks
Juice of 1 lemon, strained
½ cup margarine
1 teaspoon white pepper
Dash Tabasco sauce

Beat egg yolks and lemon juice with a whisk. Melt margarine and heat until boiling. Continue boiling for 3 minutes to cook out all water.

Gradually pour boiling margarine into egg yolk mixture, beating with whisk until all margarine is used and the egg mixture is fluffy. Beat in white pepper.

MAKES 1 CUP.

This sauce can be used with any recipe calling for Hollandaise, including our Famous New Orleans Eggs Benedict (see page 171).

Breads

❦ White Bread

4 packages (¼ ounce each) active dry yeast
2 tablespoons salt
3 tablespoons sugar
2 cups milk, warmed
¼ cup heavy cream, warmed
4 tablespoons butter, melted
8 cups plain flour
1 egg yolk
1 tablespoon milk

Mix the yeast with the salt, sugar, warm milk, warm cream, and melted butter. Stir until thoroughly dissolved. Put 6 cups of flour in a large mixing bowl and make a depression in the middle. Pour the yeast mixture into the "well" and knead it with your hands until the dough is stiff. Add more flour as necessary. Then, knead again for about 10 minutes or until the dough is smooth and elastic. Shape the dough into a ball and put in a clean bowl. Flour it lightly, cover, and let rise in a place free from drafts for about 40 minutes or until it doubles in size.

Remove the dough from the bowl, punch, and knead it again briefly to remove all the air; return the dough to the bowl, cover, and let it rise a second time until it almost doubles in bulk.

Butter four 9 × 5 × 3-inch loaf pans and divide the dough in fourths. Shape in compact loaves and place in greased pans. Cover and let rise until the dough reaches the top of the pans. Place in a preheated 400-degree oven on the lower shelf and bake for approximately 40 minutes.

Thoroughly blend an egg yolk with 1 tablespoon of milk and brush each loaf to give it a shiny, golden-brown crust.

Freezes well.

MAKES 4 LOAVES.

🍂 Wheat Bread

1 package (¼ ounce) active dry yeast
¼ cup warm water (110 degrees)
1½ cups hot water
⅓ cup brown sugar
2 teaspoons salt
3 tablespoons shortening
2 cups whole wheat flour
3¼ cups all-purpose flour, sifted

Soften the active dry yeast in the warm water. Combine the hot water, sugar, salt, and shortening. Cool to lukewarm. Stir in the wheat flour and 1 cup of the white flour, beat well. Stir in the softened yeast and add enough of the remaining white flour to make a moderately stiff dough. Turn the dough out onto a lightly floured surface and knead until satiny smooth (10 to 12 minutes). Shape the dough into a ball and place in a greased bowl, turning once to grease the surface. Cover and let rise in a warm place until it doubles in size (about 1½ hours). Punch the dough down and shape into two loaves. Place in greased loaf pans and let rise until the loaves double in size (about 1 hour and 15 minutes). Bake in a 325-degree oven for about 45 minutes. Cover loosely with foil for the last 15 minutes if the bread is browning too quickly.

MAKES 2 LOAVES.

🍂 Jean's Rolls

¾ cup Crisco
1 cup homogenized milk
2 eggs, beaten
¾ cup sugar
2 teaspoons salt
1 cup cold water
½ cup lukewarm water
2 packages (¼ ounce each) yeast
7½ cups plain flour

Scald the milk and Crisco, and then add the beaten eggs, sugar, salt, and cold water. Mix the yeast with the lukewarm milk and add it to the mixture. Add the flour 1 cup at a time. Cover and refrigerate overnight. The next day, knead with flour and cut out. Place the rolls on baking sheets and let rise until they double in size. Bake at 425 degrees until golden-brown.

MAKES 48 DINNER ROLLS.

❦ *French Toast*

3 eggs
1 cup milk
2 tablespoons Grand Marnier
1 tablespoon sugar
½ teaspoon vanilla
¼ teaspoon salt
6 slices white bread, halved
¼ cup vegetable oil or butter
Powdered sugar for topping
Honey or syrup

Beat the eggs, milk, and flavorings together in a medium-sized bowl. Arrange the bread slices in a flat dish and pour the liquid over them. Be sure that each slice is well-saturated. Cover with plastic wrap and refrigerate overnight.

When ready to prepare, heat the oil in a large skillet and brown on both sides. Top with powdered sugar and serve immediately. Serve with honey or syrup in a pitcher.

SERVES 4.

In New Orleans, this is known as Pain Perdu (Lost Bread) and may use French bread sliced in rounds.

❦ French Beignette

2 lemons
3¾ cups water, divided
3 tablespoons vanilla
2 tablespoons orange flower water
½ stick butter or margarine
4 cups self-rising flour, sifted
12 eggs
1½ cups sugar

Peel the lemons and boil the peel in ¾ cup of water. Put 3 cups of water in a large pot. Add the lemon peel water plus enough water to make 1 cup (there should be a total of 4 cups liquid now), the vanilla, orange flower water, and butter or margarine. Bring to a boil, add all the flour at once and stir well. Leave the fire on while stirring the mixture. If the fire is too high, lower it or the flour will stick to the pot and burn. The flour will stir into lumps of dough. Have a mixing pan ready so the dough will not get too cool when adding the eggs. Work the dough by hand while it is hot to keep it from getting stiff. When the dough is cool enough to handle, work in the eggs, one at a time, still by hand. After using 4 eggs, start adding 2 at a time. Sweeten with granulated sugar. Use the amount given above or to your own taste. The dough should be very smooth and creamy but also thick. Teaspoon off each doughnut into hot grease (325 degrees). Do not put too many in the pot at one time; they need to be able to turn over by themselves. Remove the doughnuts and drain. Roll in granulated sugar (powdered sugar tends to make them soggy).

This recipe was given to us by a dear friend whose grandmother was a French cook. This is a very old and famous New Orleans recipe; do not change anything.

❦ Cornbread

2 cups self-rising white cornmeal (we suggest Martha's White Cornmeal)
1¼ cups milk
1 egg
¼ cup cooking oil
1 teaspoon sugar (optional)

Preheat the oven to 450 degrees. Beat the egg with the milk and add the cooking oil. Slowly add the cornmeal and sugar. Pour the batter into a hot greased pan and bake for 15 to 20 minutes or until golden-brown.
   Use this recipe for muffins or cornbread sticks, too.

❦ Roy's Hush Puppies

2 onions, quartered
4 jalapeño peppers, sliced
1 teaspoon garlic powder
1 teaspoon salt, or to taste
¼ teaspoon white pepper
1½ cups self-rising flour
1 cup yellow cornmeal
1 teaspoon baking powder
1 teaspoon sugar
3 eggs
½ cup cold water

Place the onions and the peppers in a food processor and chop finely. Add the garlic powder, salt, and pepper, and mix well. Pour into a mixing bowl with the flour, cornmeal, baking powder, and sugar. Add the eggs and water, and mix well. Drop by teaspoons into hot peanut oil (350 degrees). Use a deep-fat fryer or pan large enough to hold enough oil to cover the hush puppies. Cook until they turn golden-brown (approximately 4 to 5 minutes) and float to the top.
   If the hush puppies are too firm, add a little water to the dough.

MAKES 30 HUSH PUPPIES.

Desserts

❦ Miss Ruby's Famous Bread Pudding

1 loaf (10 ounces) French bread, thinly sliced
3¼ cups sugar
4 eggs
1 quart milk
½ cup melted butter
1 tablespoon vanilla
1 can (15 ounces) fruit cocktail, drained
5 drops yellow food coloring

RUM SAUCE
½ cup butter
1 pound powdered sugar
2 tablespoons corn starch
¼ cup rum or whiskey
2 cups water

Slice the French bread into 1-inch slices and allow to dry out overnight.

Preheat oven to 350 degrees.

Beat the eggs with a wire whisk. Add 3 cups of the sugar, the milk, vanilla, food coloring, and melted butter, and beat well. Add the fruit cocktail and the French bread slices. Mix well by hand, leaving some pieces of the bread relatively large. Pour into a 13 × 9-inch baking dish and sprinkle the remaining sugar over the top. Bake at 350 degrees for 1½ hours or until well set. The pudding will rise up but, after removing it from the oven, it will slowly settle down. It will be a beautiful golden-brown on the outside and creamy on the inside.

To make the rum sauce, place all the ingredients, except the rum, into a saucepan. Bring to a boil and cook until it becomes a light syrup. Remove from the heat, add the rum, and mix lightly.

To serve, cut the pudding into 2½-inch squares and top with the rum sauce. At Miss Ruby's we always served the pudding bubbling hot.

When we do food shows like the annual French Quarter Festival in Jackson Square, we serve Bread Pudding and Rum Sauce piping hot from chafing pans. We have had as many as 100 people waiting in line to be served. So you can imagine how many pans of pudding our chefs have to bake. Needless to say, people love it, and we are happy to share the recipe now through our cookbook.

❦ King's Cake

1 package (¼ ounce) dry yeast
¼ cup warm water
6 tablespoons milk, scalded and cooled
4 cups plain flour, divided
1 cup melted butter
¾ cup sugar
¼ teaspoon salt
4 eggs
1 small hard plastic baby about 1 inch long
¾ cup gold, green and purple colored sugar

In a bowl dissolve the yeast in the warm water. Add the milk and enough flour, about ½ cup, to make a soft dough. In another bowl, combine the butter, sugar, salt, and eggs with an electric mixer. Remove from mixer and add the soft ball of yeast dough. Mix thoroughly. Gradually add 2½ cups of flour to make a medium dough. Place in a greased bowl and brush the top with butter. Cover with a damp cloth and set aside. Let mixture rise until it is about double in bulk, approximately 2½ to 3 hours.

Use the remaining cup of flour to knead the dough and then roll it into a rope shape. Place the dough on a 14 × 16-inch greased cookie sheet and form the "rope" of dough into an oval or round shape. Connect the ends of the dough by dampening with water. Cover and let rise for about 1 hour or until the dough doubles in bulk.

Bake in a 325-degree oven for 35 to 40 minutes, or until lightly browned. When the cake is done, raise one side of the cake and put the plastic baby into the dough on the underside of the cake. Decorate the cake by brushing with corn syrup and alternating 3-inch bands of gold, green and purple sugar.

PURPLE, GREEN, AND GOLD SUGAR
To add color, put the sugar in a jar that can be tightly capped. Add a few drops of the appropriate food coloring and shake the jar until the desired color is achieved.

You may also use the following fruit-flavored frosting on the cake if you desire.

BASIC RECIPE
8 ounces cream cheese
1 stick margarine
1 pound powdered sugar

Beat well together. Divide into three separate containers. For purple color, combine 5 drops of violet food coloring and ¼ teaspoon of grape juice. For green, add ¼ teaspoon of lemon extract to five drops of green food coloring. For gold, add 5 drops of orange food coloring and 1 teaspoon of orange liqueur. Blend well and use a pastry tube to decorate the cake.

New Orleans didn't invent the King Cake, but it has given the tradition a popularity that never achieved anywhere else. The King Cake came from Europe, where it was connected to a single date, January 6, the Epiphany. This is the day the three Wise Men visited the Christ Child bringing gifts. On Twelfth Night, to celebrate the coming of the Magi, parties were held where the focus of attention was a King Cake. In the cake was a bean (or a miniature porcelain frog or fish, or a coin), and the person who had the piece of cake with the bean was crowned king.

This tradition was transported to New Orleans, and was commonly practiced by the early 19th century. In 1870, the Twelfth Night Revelers, New Orleans' second oldest Carnival organization, selected its Queen by using a gold bean. The girl who got the gold bean was the Queen, and the others were her maids.

The King Cake's popularity has increased over the years, and it is now associated with the entire Mardi Gras season. Starting on January 6 and continuing until Fat Tuesday, New Orleanians have multiple King Cake parties. The custom is that whoever gets the baby gives the next King Cake party.

King Cakes have changed over the years. They are round or oval to represent a crown. The bean has been replaced by a porcelain baby, which was replaced with a plastic baby in the 1960s. Today, King Cakes can have different kinds of fillings, and are decorated with purple, green and gold sugar or icing. It is estimated that close to a million King Cakes are sold each Mardi Gras season here in New Orleans.

🍋 Chocolate Cheesecake

CRUST
1½ cups graham cracker crumbs
2 tablespoons sugar
¼ teaspoon ground cinnamon
¼ cup margarine or butter, melted

FILLING
1½ cups semi-sweet chocolate morsels
2 eggs
1 cup sugar
1 carton (8 ounces) sour cream
2 packages (8 ounces each) cream cheese, softened
2 tablespoons butter or margarine, melted

Combine all the crust ingredients and blend well. Firmly press into the bottom of a 10-inch springform pan. Set aside.

Melt the chocolate in the top of a double boiler over hot water. Set aside.

Combine the eggs, sugar, and sour cream. Blend for 1 minute using an electric mixer. Gradually add the melted chocolate and cream cheese while continuing to blend. Add the melted butter and blend well. Pour the mixture into the crust and bake at 325 degrees for 45 minutes, or until the cheesecake is set in the center.

Cool at room temperature for at least 1 hour. Chill at least 6 hours. Remove sides of the springform pan. Top with whipped cream before serving.

SERVES 10 TO 12.

A springform pan is a cheesecake pan available at any kitchen shop.

❦ *Hummingbird Cake*

3 cups all-purpose flour
2 cups sugar
1 teaspoon salt
1 teaspoon baking soda
1 teaspoon cinnamon
3 eggs, beaten
1½ cups vegetable oil
1½ teaspoons vanilla
1 can (8 ounces) crushed pineapple (do not drain)
1 cup chopped pecans
2 cups ripe bananas, mashed

FROSTING
1 package (8 ounces) cream cheese, softened
1 stick margarine or butter
2 pounds powdered sugar
2 teaspoons vanilla
1 cup pecans, chopped
4 tablespoons evaporated milk

Preheat the oven to 350 degrees.

Combine the dry ingredients (except the pecans) in a large bowl. Add the eggs and oil until the dry ingredients are moistened. *Do not beat*. Stir in the vanilla, pineapple, pecans, and bananas. Blend well. Pour into 4 greased and floured 9-inch cake pans. Bake at 350 degrees for 30 to 35 minutes. Cool the layers well and then frost.

For frosting, mix together the cream cheese and margarine. Add the powdered sugar, milk, and vanilla. Beat until creamy. Add the pecans and stir. Spread between the layers, around the sides and over the top of the cake.

SERVES 12.

🍒 Banana Cake

3½ cups cake flour, sifted
¾ teaspoon salt
¾ teaspoon baking powder
¾ cup shortening
2¼ cups sugar
3 eggs, slightly beaten
1½ cups ripe bananas, mashed
1½ teaspoons vanilla
1½ teaspoons baking soda
½ cup buttermilk
1 cup walnuts, chopped

FROSTING
1 cup margarine
1 package (8 ounces) cream cheese
1 cup ripe bananas, mashed
1 teaspoon vanilla
2 pounds powdered sugar
1 ounce evaporated milk

Preheat the oven to 350 degrees. Grease and flour three 9-inch cake pans.

Sift the flour, salt, and baking powder together. In a mixing bowl, cream the shortening and sugar together until light and fluffy. Stir in the eggs, bananas, and vanilla. Dissolve the baking soda in the buttermilk and add alternately with the flour mixture, beating well. After each addition of flour or buttermilk, add some walnuts. Pour the batter into the pans. Bake for 25 to 30 minutes at 350 degrees. Cool for 5 minutes before removing from the pans.

For the frosting, cream the margarine, cream cheese, bananas, and vanilla together. Beat until smooth. Add the sugar and beat until smooth. If the icing is a little too thick, thin with some milk. Spread the frosting between the layers, around the sides and over the top of the cake.

❦ Carrot Cake

1 cup Crisco oil
2 cups grated carrots
4 eggs, separated
2 cups sugar
½ teaspoon salt
2 teaspoons baking powder
2 teaspoons baking soda
2 teaspoons cinnamon
3 cups cake flour, sifted
½ cup walnuts, chopped

FROSTING
2 sticks margarine or butter
1 package (8 ounces) cream cheese
1 teaspoon vanilla
2 pounds powdered sugar
¼ cup evaporated milk
1 cup walnuts, chopped

Combine the oil, carrots, and egg yolks, and mix thoroughly. Blend the sugar, salt, baking powder, baking soda, and cinnamon together. Add to the first mixture. Add the flour, saving a small amount to mix with the nuts. Beat the egg whites until stiff and add the nuts. Stir both mixtures together well and pour into 3 greased and floured cake pans. Bake at 350 degrees for 30 minutes.

For the frosting, mix the margarine and cream cheese together until creamy. Add the vanilla, powdered sugar, and milk. Beat well and then add the nuts. Mix well. If the icing is too thick, thin with a little milk. Spread the frosting between the layers, around the sides and over the top of the carrot cake.

This is one of the most popular cakes at Miss Ruby's.

❦ Old-Fashioned Pound Cake

3 cups sugar
2 sticks butter or margarine
½ cup Crisco shortening
6 eggs
3 cups cake flour
½ teaspoon baking powder (sift together with the flour)
1 cup milk
1 teaspoon vanilla
2 teaspoons lemon extract

Preheat oven to 300 degrees.

Cream together the sugar, butter, and Crisco. Add the eggs one at a time, blending well after each addition. Add the flour and baking powder slowly, alternating with the milk, until the mixture is well-beaten. Add the vanilla and lemon extract. Mix well. Pour into a tube cake pan and bake at 300 degrees for 1 hour and 25 minutes. Cool in the pan for 10 minutes and then turn out to finish cooling.

Since this is a plain cake, it can be served with rum sauce and ice cream.

With fresh Louisiana strawberries and lots of whipped cream, this cake becomes Strawberry Shortcake.

❦ Sour Cream Pound Cake

¼ teaspoon baking soda
1 cup sour cream
1 stick butter
1 stick margarine
3 cups sugar
6 eggs
3 cups sifted cake flour
1 teaspoon lemon extract
1 teaspoon vanilla

Preheat the oven to 325 degrees.

Add the baking soda to the sour cream and let stand. Cream together the butter, margarine, and sugar with an electric mixer. Beat for a long time until well creamed. Add the eggs one at a time, beating well after each addition. Mix in the flour with an electric mixer on low speed. Add the lemon extract and vanilla. Add the sour cream mixture. Stir until well-blended. Pour into a greased and floured tube pan. Bake at 325 degrees for 1 hour and 25 minutes. Cool in the pan for 10 minutes and then turn out to finish cooling.

SERVES 12 TO 15.

❧ *Banana Split Cake*

2 sticks margarine
2 cups graham cracker crumbs
2 eggs
2 cups powdered sugar
6 bananas
1 can (15 ounces) crushed pineapple, drained
1 container (16 ounces) Cool Whip
1 cup chopped nuts
1 cup maraschino cherries, chopped

Combine 1 stick of margarine with the graham cracker crumbs. Press into a 14 × 9 × 2-inch Pyrex dish. Beat the eggs, the other stick of margarine, and the sugar together for 15 minutes with an electric mixer. Spread over the graham cracker crumb shell. Slice the bananas and arrange over the mixture. Spread the pineapple over the bananas. Top with Cool Whip. Sprinkle with the nuts and place the cherries on top. Let the cake set all day or overnight. This cake must be kept in the refrigerator at all times because of the fruit and egg mixture. To serve, cut in 2-inch squares.

This dessert is not only good but makes a beautiful dessert for parties, and you are guaranteed to win friends. Miss Jean always makes this cake for Dr. Ralph Lupin's parties because it was his favorite.

🍎 Fresh Apple Pound Cake

1½ cups corn oil
2 cups sugar
3 eggs
3 cups all-purpose flour
1 teaspoon baking soda
1 teaspoon salt
1 teaspoon ground cinnamon
1 teaspoon ground nutmeg
2 teaspoons vanilla
3 cups apples, finely chopped
1 cup pecans, chopped
½ cup coconut (optional)

ICING
1½ cups brown sugar
½ cup butter
1 cup evaporated milk
½ cup chopped pecans
½ cup coconut

Preheat the oven to 350 degrees.

Blend the corn oil, sugar, and eggs well. Sift the flour, baking soda, salt and cinnamon together. Add to the sugar and egg mixture, and mix well. Add the vanilla, apples, pecans and coconut. Blend well. Pour into a greased and floured tube pan. Bake at 350 degrees for 1 hour and 15 minutes. Cool for 10 minutes in the pan before turning out.

For the icing, blend the brown sugar, butter, and evaporated milk in a saucepan, and cook until thickened. Add the coconut and pecans and pour over the cake.

SERVES 12 TO 15.

❦ Red Velvet Cake

1½ cups sugar
1¼ cups butter or margarine
3 eggs
1 tablespoon vinegar
1 tablespoon cocoa
1 ounce red food coloring
2½ cups cake flour
½ teaspoon salt
1½ teaspoons baking soda
¼ teaspoon baking powder
1 cup buttermilk
1 teaspoon vanilla

FROSTING
1 package (8 ounces) cream cheese
1 cup pecans, chopped
2 sticks margarine or butter
2 boxes (16 ounces each) powdered sugar
1 teaspoon vanilla
5 tablespoons milk or evaporated milk

Preheat the oven to 350 degrees.

Cream together the sugar, butter, and eggs. Make a paste of the vinegar, cocoa, and food coloring. Add to the creamed mixture. Mix well. Add the dry ingredients, alternating with the buttermilk and mixing well after each addition. Add the vanilla and blend well. Pour into three greased and floured 9-inch cake pans. Bake at 350 degrees for 30 minutes.

For the frosting, cream the margarine and cream cheese together until fluffy. Add the powdered sugar, vanilla, and milk. Mix well. Add the pecans and mix well. Spread the frosting between the layers, around the sides and over the top of the cake.

Makes a beautiful cake, especially for the Christmas holidays.

🍎 Easy Amaretto Cake

CAKE
1 box Duncan Hines butter cake mix
1 box instant vanilla pudding
4 eggs
½ cup amaretto liqueur
½ cup water

GLAZE
1 cup powdered sugar
¼ cup amaretto liqueur
1 stick margarine

Preheat the oven to 350 degrees. Grease and flour a tube cake pan.

Mix all the cake ingredients together with an electric mixer for 2 to 3 minutes. Pour the batter into the tube pan. Bake at 350 degrees for 45 to 50 minutes.

For the glaze, bring the ingredients to a boil for 3 minutes. While the cake is warm and still in the pan, pour half the glaze over the cake. Let stand 20 minutes. Take the cake out of pan and pour the remaining glaze over the bottom of the cake.

SERVES 10 TO 12.

🍎 Yellow Cake

1 cup margarine or butter
2 cups sugar
4 egg yolks
1 cup milk
1 teaspoon vanilla
3 cups cake flour
3 teaspoons baking powder
¼ teaspoon salt
4 egg whites, beaten stiff

Preheat the oven to 350 degrees. Grease and flour three 10-inch cake pans.

Cream the butter and sugar together until light and creamy. Add the egg yolks one at a time, beating well after each addition. Add the vanilla and milk. Alternately add the milk and the dry ingredients into the creamed mixture. Fold in the beaten egg whites. Pour the batter into the cake pans. Bake at 350 degrees for 40 minutes.

SERVES 12.

This yellow cake is the basis for several different kinds of cakes. For instance, to make a coconut cake, simply use the Seven-Minute Frosting (see page 223) and sprinkle coconut over frosting between the layers, spread coconut on frosting around the sides, and cover the frosting on top of the cake with coconut as well.

❦ *Jean's Lemon Fruit Cake*

1 pound butter, creamed
1 box (16 ounces) light brown sugar
6 eggs
4 cups all purpose flour
2 ounces lemon extract
½ pound candied pineapple, chopped
½ pound red and green cherries, chopped
4 cups pecans, chopped

Combine all the ingredients and mix well. Pour into a 10-inch tube pan and refrigerate at least 12 hours.

Bake at 325 degrees for 1½ hours.

SERVES 12 TO 15.

This cake keeps well and freezes well. It can be soaked in your favorite brandy and wrapped tightly in plastic wrap. The longer it sets, the better it tastes.

🍂 Banana Nut Bread

½ cup Crisco shortening
1 cup sugar
2 eggs, well-beaten
2 cups all purpose flour
½ teaspoon salt
1 teaspoon vanilla
1 teaspoon baking soda
3 large very ripe bananas
½ cup pecans or walnuts, chopped

Preheat the oven to 350 degrees. Grease and flour a loaf pan.

Cream the shortening and sugar together. Add the eggs and the remaining ingredients and, using an electric mixer, mix together well. Pour into the loaf pan and bake at 350 degrees for 1 hour.

SERVES 8 TO 10.

🍂 Simple Rum Cake

CAKE
½ cup chopped pecans
1 small box instant vanilla pudding
½ cup rum
½ cup water
4 eggs
½ cup Crisco oil
1 package yellow cake mix (we prefer Duncan Hines)

GLAZE
1 cup sugar
½ cup butter
¼ cup rum
¼ cup water

Preheat the oven to 350 degrees. Grease and flour a Bundt cake pan. Sprinkle the pecans in the bottom of the pan.

Beat together the remaining cake ingredients with an electric mixer for 2 to 3 minutes. Pour the batter into the cake pan. Bake at 350 degrees for 1 hour. Remove from the oven. Pour the glaze over the cake while still hot. Cool in the pan for 15 minutes and then turn out onto a plate.

To make the glaze, boil the ingredients together for 2 to 3 minutes.

SERVES 10 TO 12.

❧ Devil's Food Cake

3 squares (1 ounce each) unsweetened chocolate
⅔ cup Crisco shortening
2¼ cups sifted cake flour
2 cups sugar
1 teaspoon salt
1 teaspoon baking soda
1 teaspoon baking powder
1¼ cups milk, divided
3 eggs
1 teaspoon red food coloring

Preheat the oven to 350 degrees.

Melt the chocolate in the top of a double boiler and set aside to cool.

Combine the shortening, flour, sugar, salt, baking soda, and baking powder in a bowl, and blend well. Add ½ cup milk and mix. Beat 2 minutes at medium speed with an electric mixer. Add the rest of the milk, the eggs, food coloring and chocolate. Beat 2 minutes longer. Pour into three lightly greased and floured cake pans and bake at 350 degrees for 30 to 35 minutes.

Frost the layers with Basic Seven-Minute Frosting (see page 223). Or alternate with Chocolate Fudge Frosting for a special effect (see page 223).

SERVES 10 TO 12.

❦ Heavenly Hash Cake

4 eggs
2 sticks margarine, melted
2 cups sugar
4 tablespoons cocoa
2 cups chopped pecans
2 teaspoons vanilla
1½ cups self-rising flour
1½ cups miniature marshmallows

FROSTING
1 stick margarine
3 tablespoons cocoa
½ cup evaporated milk
1 box (16 ounces) powdered sugar
1 teaspoon vanilla

Preheat the oven to 325 degrees.

Cream together the margarine, sugar, and eggs. Add the cocoa, nuts, vanilla, and flour. Mix well. Pour into a greased and floured, 9 × 12-inch glass baking dish. Bake at 325 degrees for approximately 45 minutes. While the cake is still hot, top with the marshmallows and return to the oven long enough for the marshmallows to puff up.

Meanwhile, melt the margarine. Add the cocoa and remove from the heat. Add the remaining frosting ingredients. Beat until smooth. Pour the frosting over the cake and put back into the oven for 5 more minutes.

To serve, cut into 2- to 3-inch squares.

SERVES 10.

❦ Italian Cream Cake

1 stick margarine
½ cup shortening
2 cups sugar
5 egg yolks
2 cups all-purpose flour
1 teaspoon baking soda
1 cup buttermilk
1 can (7 ounces) coconut
1 cup chopped pecans
1 teaspoon vanilla
5 egg whites, beaten until stiff

FROSTING
1 package (8 ounces) cream cheese
2 boxes (16 ounces each) powdered sugar
1 cup nuts, chopped
1 stick margarine
1 teaspoon vanilla
¼ cup evaporated milk

Preheat the oven to 350 degrees.

Cream together the margarine and shortening. Add the sugar and egg yolks. Mix well. Sift together the flour and baking soda and add alternately with the buttermilk, blending well with each addition. Add the coconut, nuts, and vanilla, and mix well. Fold in the egg whites. Pour into three greased and floured 9-inch cake pans. Bake at 350 degrees for 25 minutes.

For the frosting, mix all the ingredients together and beat until very smooth. Spread between the layers, around the sides and over the top of the cake.

SERVES 10 TO 12.

❧ *Mississippi Mud Cake*

2 sticks margarine
½ cup cocoa
2 cups sugar
4 eggs, slightly beaten
1½ cups all-purpose flour
Pinch of salt
1½ cups pecans, chopped
1 teaspoon vanilla
1 package (16 ounces) miniature marshmallows

TOPPING
1 box (16 ounces) powdered sugar
⅓ cup milk
⅓ cup cocoa
½ stick margarine

Melt the margarine and cocoa together. Remove from the heat and stir in the sugar and eggs. Blend until smooth. Add the flour, salt, nuts, and vanilla. Mix well. Spread in a greased 13 × 9-inch pan. Bake at 350 degrees for 35 to 45 minutes. Sprinkle the marshmallows on top of the cake while it's hot.

Combine all the topping ingredients in a mixing bowl. Blend well. Pour over the cake while the cake is still warm. With the back of a spoon, spread the frosting in circles to make it look "muddy."

To serve, cut into 2- to 3-inch squares.

SERVES 10.

🦋 German Chocolate Cake

4 eggs, separated
1 cup butter
2 cups sugar
1 teaspoon baking soda
1 cup buttermilk, divided
2½ cups cake flour
1 package (4 ounces) German chocolate bar, dissolved in ½ cup hot water
¼ teaspoon salt
1 teaspoon vanilla

FROSTING
2 cups sugar
1 cup margarine
2 cups evaporated milk
4 egg yolks, beaten
2 teaspoons vanilla
2 cups grated coconut
2 cups chopped pecans

Preheat the oven to 350 degrees.

Beat the egg whites until stiff. Cream the margarine together with the sugar. Add the egg yolks one at a time and beat well with each addition. Dissolve the baking soda in ½ cup of buttermilk and add to the mixture. Stir well. Add the flour, chocolate, salt, vanilla, and remaining buttermilk. Beat well. Fold in the egg whites. Pour into three 9-inch greased and floured cake pans. Bake at 350 degrees for 35 minutes. Allow the layers to cool well before you try to handle them, or they will break.

For the frosting, mix the sugar, margarine, milk, and beaten egg yolks in a saucepan. Beat together well and cook over medium heat until thickened. Add the vanilla, coconut and pecans and allow to cool. Frost between the layers, around the sides and on the top of the cake.

SERVES 12 TO 14.

🍎 Key Lime Pie

1¼ cups sugar
3 tablespoons flour
3 tablespoons cornstarch
¼ teaspoon salt
2 cups boiling water
5 egg yolks
¼ cup lime juice, freshly squeezed
1 teaspoon lime peel, freshly grated
2 tablespoons butter
10-inch pie shell, baked and cooled

MERINGUE
5 egg whites
1 teaspoon cream of tartar
5 tablespoons sugar

Preheat the oven to 400 degrees. Blend the sugar, flour, cornstarch, salt, and boiling water in s saucepan over medium heat, stirring constantly. Remove from the heat.

Beat the egg yolks slightly. Add ¼ cup of the custard to the yolks and blend well. Combine the egg yolks with the rest of the custard mixture and return to the heat. Cook slowly for 2 minutes. Add the lime juice, lime peel, and butter. Remove from the heat and stir until the butter is melted.

Beat the egg whites and cream of tartar until the egg whites begin to hold their shape. Continue beating and gradually add the sugar. Beat until stiff peaks form.

Fold 1 cup of the meringue into the filling. Pour the filling into the pie crust. Spread the rest of the meringue over the top of the pie, sealing the edges. Bake at 400 degrees for 15 minutes, or until golden-brown.

This is a very popular dessert for St. Patrick's Day. If you want to color the pie green, add 3 drops of green food coloring.

❦ Homemade Vanilla Ice Cream

4 large eggs
2¼ cups sugar
½ teaspoon salt
1 pint light cream
1 pint whipping cream
2 pints half-and-half
8 teaspoons vanilla

Beat the eggs and add the sugar gradually. Beat until the mixture is very stiff. Add the remaining ingredients and mix thoroughly. Pour into a 1-gallon container and freeze.

This is called the hill country ice cream because the recipe came from the Texas hill country.

❦ Seven-Layer Cookies

1 stick margarine, melted
1½ cups graham cracker crumbs
1 cup coconut
1 package (6 ounces) chocolate chips
1 package (6 ounces) butterscotch chips
1 can Eagle Brand condensed milk
1 cup pecans, chopped

Preheat the oven to 350 degrees.

In a 9 × 13-inch pan, pour the melted margarine over the graham cracker crumbs. Mix well, and press to the sides and bottom of the pan.

Layer the remaining ingredients in this order: Coconut, chocolate chips, and butterscotch chips. Then, pour the condensed milk over the layered ingredients and sprinkle with the pecans. Bake at 350 degrees for 30 minutes. Allow to cool and then cut into squares.

I have always had a problem keeping this dessert, because the chef calls it his "energy bar."

❦ Jean's Fruit Cake Cookies

2 sticks margarine or butter
1 cup light brown sugar
3 eggs
¾ cup white raisins
2 cups pecans, chopped
6 slices green candied pineapple, chopped
½ pound red candied cherries, chopped
2 cups dates, chopped
½ cup bourbon or milk
3 cups all-purpose flour
1 teaspoon cinnamon
½ teaspoon baking soda
Pinch salt

Cream the margarine and sugar together well. Add all the remaining ingredients and mix well. Chill overnight. Drop onto greased cookie sheets and bake at 350 degrees for approximately 20 minutes.

This recipe can be made ahead of time and stored in an airtight container.

Miss Jean always passed these out to her customers at Christmas time. Everyone looked forward to them, as a special treat.

❦ Oatmeal Cookies

1¼ cups margarine or butter, at room temperature
¾ cup brown sugar, firmly packed
½ cup sugar
1 egg
1 teaspoon vanilla
1½ cups all-purpose flour
1 teaspoon baking soda
1 teaspoon salt
1 teaspoon cinnamon (optional)
3 cups old-fashioned oats, uncooked (may substitute quick oats)

Preheat the oven to 375 degrees.

Beat the margarine or butter and sugar together until fluffy. Beat the egg and vanilla together. Combine the flour, baking soda, salt, and cinnamon. Add both to the margarine mixture. Mix well. Stir in the oats and mix well.

Drop by rounded tablespoons onto ungreased cookie sheets. Bake at 375 degrees for 12 minutes, or until golden-brown (if a chewy cookie is preferred, bake for only 8 to 9 minutes). Cool on the cookie sheets for a minute before removing and then continue to cool on a wire rack. Store in airtight containers. These cookies will keep for a week or more.

There are many variations to this basic oatmeal cookie recipe, all of which are delicious. Add a cup of raisins, chopped nuts, semisweet chocolate chips, or butterscotch chips to change the flavor.

🦃 *Pecan Pralines*

1 cup Pet milk
3 cups sugar
1 stick butter
6 tablespoons sugar (to caramelize)
 2 teaspoons vanilla
½ teaspoon baking soda
1 cup pecans

Bring the milk, 3 cups of sugar, and butter to a boil, stirring continuously for 5 minutes until the mixture forms a soft ball. While the mixture is coming to a boil, caramelize the 6 tablespoons of sugar and add it to the mixture, along with the vanilla. (Be careful or the caramelized sugar will splash and burn you.) Remove from the heat, fold in the baking soda and set aside for 5 minutes. Add the pecans and stir until you think is is time to pour — when they get somewhat heavy but not cool. You will learn this from practice. Drop the candy from a spoon onto waxed paper. If the pralines are poured too late, they will turn to sugar just as fudge does.

❦ Chocolate Fudge Cake

1 cup margarine or butter
2 cups sugar
5 eggs
2½ cups all-purpose flour
½ cup cocoa
1 cup buttermilk
1 teaspoon baking soda
2 tablespoons water

Preheat the oven to 350 degrees.

Cream the margarine or butter thoroughly with the sugar. Add the eggs one at a time, beating well after each addition. Sift the flour and cocoa together. Add the flour mixture alternately with the buttermilk, beating until smooth after each addition. Dissolve the baking soda in water and add to the mixture. Mix well. Turn the mixture into three greased and floured layer cake pans. Bake at 350 degrees for approximately 30 minutes, or until the cake springs back in the middle when tested.

Cool well before frosting. Frost with Chocolate Fudge Frosting (see following recipe).

> *At Miss Ruby's we called this our "Wake Cake" because, in New Orleans the custom of holding watch over the body of the deceased is retained. Food and beverage are taken to be served at a wake, and many people order this cake to take to the family. As a result, many people call in wanting to place special take-out orders for this cake.*

❦ Chocolate Fudge Frosting

½ pound margarine
½ cup cocoa
2 pounds powdered sugar
¼ cup evaporated milk
1 tablespoon vanilla

Cream the butter and cocoa together. Add the powdered sugar, vanilla, and evaporated milk. Beat with an electric mixer for 5 minutes or until very creamy. Spread over the top and sides of your cake.

For a special effect, reserve ½ cup of the frosting. Place in a double boiler and heat for 2 minutes. Drizzle around the edge of the cake. Heating the frosting makes it darker in color and creates a pretty look.

❦ Seven-Minute Frosting

3 egg whites
1½ cups granulated sugar
1 tablespoon light corn syrup (Karo White)
½ teaspoon cream of tartar
⅓ cup cold water
Dash salt
1 teaspoon vanilla

Place all the ingredients except the vanilla in the top of a double boiler (do not place over boiling water at this time). Beat 1 minute at medium speed with an electric mixer. Place the top of the double boiler over boiling water (it should not touch the water). Cook while beating constantly until the frosting forms stiff peaks (about 7 minutes). Remove from the water and add the vanilla. Beat for 2 minutes, or until the mixture has reached spreading consistency. Frost the sides and top of your cake.

For added effect, melt 1 tablespoon of shortening and 1 tablespoon of cocoa together to make a chocolate syrup. Drizzle over the top and sides of your cake.

We use this on Devil's Food Cake (see page 213) and Coconut Cake (see Yellow Cake recipe, page 210).

❦ Cheesecake

CRUST
1 cup graham cracker crumbs
¾ cup nuts, finely chopped
2 tablespoons margarine, melted

FILLING
4 packages (8 ounces) cream cheese
4 eggs
1¼ cups sugar
1 tablespoon lemon juice, freshly squeezed

TOPPING
¼ cup sugar
1 cup sour cream
1 teaspoon vanilla

Preheat the oven to 350 degrees.

Combine the crust ingredients and blend well. With a spoon, press the mixture into the bottom of a springform pan until a consistently even crust forms. Bake at 350 degrees for 5 minutes.

In a mixing bowl, combine all the filling ingredients and mix well. Pour into the crust and bake at 350 degrees for 55 minutes.

Meanwhile, blend together the topping ingredients. Remove the cheesecake from the oven and spread on the topping mixture. Bake another 10 minutes.

This dessert should be baked 1 day ahead.

SERVES 12 TO 15.

This recipe is very rich, so serve thin slices. It is delicious served with raspberry, strawberry, or cherry topping.

❦ Perfect Pie Crust

2 cups all purpose flour
¼ teaspoon salt
½ cup Crisco shortening
5 tablespoons ice water

Mix the shortening, flour, and salt together with a fork. Gradually add the water. Mix until the dough holds together. Turn out onto a floured board and roll out. Put the dough in a pie plate and cut excess pastry from the edges. Bake at 375 degrees for 15 minutes. Prick the shell with a fork and bake another 4 minutes.

❦ Chocolate Mousse

6 ounces semisweet chocolate
2½ tablespoons Kahlua liqueur
1 tablespoon orange juice
2 large egg yolks
2 large eggs
1 teaspoon vanilla
¼ cup sugar
1 cup heavy cream

Melt the chocolate in the Kahlua and orange juice over very low heat. Set aside.

Put the egg yolks, eggs, vanilla, and sugar into a blender. Blend for 2 minutes at medium-high speed. Add the heavy cream and blend another 30 seconds. Add the melted chocolate mixture and blend until smooth. Pour into a parfait or stemmed saucer champagne glass. Refrigerate.

This is the smoothest, richest chocolate mousse you have ever tasted.

❦ Pecan Pie

4 eggs, beaten
½ cup sugar
1 cup white Karo syrup
2 tablespoons margarine or butter, melted
Dash of salt
1 teaspoon vanilla
1 cup pecans, coarsely chopped
10-inch unbaked pie shell

Preheat the oven to 350 degrees.
    Beat all the ingredients together. Add the pecans and mix well. Pour into the pie shell. Bake at 350 degrees for 45 minutes.

    SERVES 8.

Miss Ruby likes to use about 12 whole pecan halves to decorate the top of the pie, first dipping the pecans in the filling before cooking to moisten them.

❦ Miss Jean's World-Famous Peanut Butter Pie

FILLING
1 cup sugar
⅓ cup flour
¼ teaspoon salt
2 cups milk
5 eggs
¼ cup margarine or butter
1 teaspoon vanilla
½ cup Jif Extra-Crunchy Peanut Butter
10-inch pie shell, baked and cooled

MERINGUE
5 egg whites
1 teaspoon cream of tartar
5 tablespoons sugar

½ cup dry-roasted peanuts, chopped

Preheat the oven to 350 degrees.

In a heavy 3-quart saucepan, combine the sugar, flour, salt, milk, and eggs. Mix well. Place over medium heat, and beat with an electric hand mixer to keep from lumping and sticking until the mixture thickens. After it thickens, add the margarine or butter, vanilla, and peanut butter. Mix together well and cook for another minute.

Pour into the pie shell.

In a mixing bowl, combine the egg whites, cream of tartar, and sugar. Beat with an electric hand mixer until stiff. Spread over the pie, sealing the edge to keep the meringue from shrinking and pulling away from the crust. Leave the meringue in peaks to make a pretty presentation. Sprinkle the peanuts over the meringue. Bake at 350 degrees until golden-brown all over (this will make the meringue stiff enough to cut).

The big secret is to spread the meringue over the pie while the filling is still warm. Miss Jean says this keeps the meringue from weeping.

SERVES 8.

Customers and leading food magazines have asked for this recipe frequently over the past 5 years. This is the first time we have shared it with anyone.

❦ Banana Cream Pie

1 cup sugar
½ cup flour
2 cups milk
½ teaspoon salt
4 egg yolks
1 stick margarine
1 teaspoon vanilla
2 very ripe bananas, thinly sliced
10-inch pie shell, baked and cooled

MERINGUE
4 egg whites
½ teaspoon cream of tartar
5 tablespoons sugar

Preheat the oven to 350 degrees.

In a 2-quart saucepan, mix together the sugar, flour, milk, salt, and egg yolks over medium heat. Beat with an electric mixer until thickened. Add the margarine and vanilla, and continue cooking for 1 minute. Pour half the filling into the pie shell. Place a layer of sliced bananas over the filling. Pour in the rest of the filling.

Beat the egg whites and cream of tartar until stiff but not dry. Slowly add the sugar and continue beating until stiff, dry peaks form. Spread the meringue over the top of the pie, sealing the edges. Bake at 350 degrees for 15 minutes, or until golden-brown.

SERVES 8.

❦ Coconut Cream Pie

FILLING
1 cup sugar
⅓ cup flour (or 3 tablespoons cornstarch)
½ teaspoon salt
2 cups milk
4 egg yolks
1 stick margarine or butter
1 teaspoon vanilla
¾ cup coconut, divided
10-inch pie shell, baked and cooled

MERINGUE
4 egg whites
½ teaspoon cream of tartar
4 tablespoons sugar

Preheat the oven to 350 degrees.

In a saucepan, beat together the filling ingredients with an electric mixer, except the coconut. Cook over medium heat, stirring constantly, until mixture thickens. Add ½ cup coconut and stir well. Pour into pie shell.

Beat the egg whites and cream of tartar until stiff but not dry. Add the sugar until stiff. Spread over the pie and seal the edges. Sprinkle the remaining coconut on top. Bake at 350 degrees for 25 minutes, or until the meringue is browned and the coconut is toasted.

SERVES 8.

❦ Chocolate Pie

FILLING
4 egg yolks, well-beaten
4 tablespoons flour
1 cup sugar
4 tablespoons cocoa
2 cups milk
1 stick margarine or butter
1 teaspoon vanilla
10-inch pie shell, baked and cooled

MERINGUE
4 egg whites
½ teaspoon cream of tartar
6 tablespoons sugar

Preheat the oven to 350 degrees.

In a saucepan, beat together all the filling ingredients. Cook over medium heat, stirring constantly, until thickened. Pour into the pie shell.

Beat together the egg whites with the cream of tartar until soft peaks form. Do not overbeat the whites before adding the sugar or the meringue will leak, making the top of the pie moist. Gradually add the sugar, beating until the meringue is stiff. Spread over the top of the pie, sealing the edge to keep the meringue from pulling away from the crust. Bake at 350 degrees for 12 to 15 minutes.

SERVES 8.

Miss Jean's secret to a perfect meringue is to put the meringue on the pie while the filling is still warm. Use the proper heat and bake until well-browned; this makes the meringue a little drier, which helps it last longer.

❧ Bread Pudding Custard-Style

1 cup seedless raisins
12 eggs
1 quart milk, scalded
½ pound butter, melted
1 can (12 ounces) evaporated milk
1 pound sugar
2 tablespoons vanilla
½ loaf French bread
½ teaspoon cinnamon
¼ teaspoon nutmeg

RUM SAUCE
1 cup granulated sugar
½ pound butter
¼ cup rum

Preheat the oven to 350 degrees. Boil the raisins until they puff up. Drain them and set aside.

In a large mixing bowl, combine the eggs, milk, butter, evaporated milk, sugar, and vanilla. Beat well. Soak the bread in cold water. Squeeze all the water from the bread. Add the bread to the mixture and mix well. Put into a large baking pan. Sprinkle the raisins, cinnamon, and nutmeg over the top. Bake at 350 degrees for about 1½ hours, or until the pudding is set when you shake the pan.

For the rum sauce, cook all the sauce ingredients over low heat for 15 minutes. Serve hot over the warm bread pudding.

SERVES 10 TO 12.

❦ Banana Pudding

1 cup sugar
¼ cup flour
Dash salt
2 cups milk
4 egg yolks
1 stick margarine or butter
1 teaspoon vanilla
4 ripe bananas, sliced
1 box (10 ounces) vanilla wafers

MERINGUE
4 egg whites
1 teaspoon cream of tartar
4 tablespoons sugar

In a 3-quart saucepan, combine the sugar, flour, salt, milk, and egg yolks. Mix well. Cook over medium heat, stirring constantly, for approximately 15 minutes, or until the mixture thickens. Add the margarine (or butter) and the vanilla. Stir well.

In a 13 × 9-inch baking dish, place a layer of vanilla wafers and then a layer of sliced bananas. Pour the pudding over the bananas and wafers.

Beat the egg whites with the cream of tartar until stiff, but not dry. Gradually add the sugar, beating continuously until very stiff. Spread over the pudding. Bake at 350 degrees until golden-brown.

❦ Sweet Potato Pie

4 medium sweet potatoes, boiled in water until tender
2 eggs
1 cup evaporated milk
1¼ cups sugar
½ cup margarine or butter, melted
1 teaspoon vanilla
1 tablespoon lemon juice or lemon extract
½ teaspoon cinnamon
Dash of salt
10-inch pie shell, unbaked

Preheat the oven to 350 degrees.

Remove the skins and mash the potatoes. Beat together the eggs, milk, sugar, butter, vanilla, lemon juice, and cinnamon. Add the mashed sweet potatoes and mix well. Pour into the pie shell. Bake at 350 degrees for approximately 40 minutes.

SERVES 8.

This is very good topped with whipped cream.

❦ Index

❦ *Order Form*

You may order additional copies of *Miss Ruby's Southern Creole and Cajun Cuisine* by writing to:

Ruby Wilkinson
940 Royal St.
Box 240
New Orleans, La. 70116

Name _____

Address _____

City, State, Zip _____

_____ copies @ $19.95 each _____

Louisiana residents add 9% sales tax _____

$2.50 shipping and handling _____

TOTAL _____

❑ Payment enclosed

❑ Charge to:

Visa # _____ Exp. Date _____

MasterCard # _____ Exp. Date _____

Signature _____

SHIP TO (if different from name and address above):

Name _____

Address _____

City, State, Zip _____